The Power of a Collective Mindset

THE POWER OF A COLLECTIVE MINDSET

"How an Invisible Virus Has Held Our Generation Back"

BY: S. OLAMILEKAN ISREAL

THE POWER OF A COLLECTIVE MINDSET

Copyright © 2024 By S. Olamilekan Isreal

All rights reserved.

S. Olamilekan Isreal

The President, The Light of Israel services

Website: www.olamilekanisreal.com

Editor: Mr. Kolade Gbolagade

ISBN:978-978-770-576-6

Table of Contents

PREFACE

In a world often marked by division and misunderstanding, "The Power of a Collective Mindset" is a crucial guide to understanding the forces shaping our behaviour, decisions, and the ultimate success or failure of our communities and organisations. This book explores the psychology behind why we act the way we do, both individually and collectively, and offers practical strategies for bridging gaps, fostering genuine connections, and unlocking the collective potential within us all.

Through real-world examples, cutting-edge research, and practical strategies, we will delve into the different ways in which a collective mindset can:

1. Drive social change and innovation
2. Foster empathy and understanding
3. Unlock collective intelligence and creativity
4. Overcome seemingly insurmountable challenges

This book is for anyone seeking to:

1. Understand the hidden forces shaping our world
2. Tap into the collective potential of their team, organisation, or community
3. Harness the power of shared intention to drive meaningful progress

Join me on this journey into the heart of a collective mindset. Let us unlock the limitless potential that awaits when we come together with a shared purpose.

My motivation for writing this book stems from a deep-seated curiosity and concern about the patterns that I have observed in people, societies, and organisations. Growing up, I was often puzzled by the stark differences in behaviour across generations, the rigid mindsets some societies cling to, and the contrast between stagnant organisations and those thriving with creativity and innovation. It became clear that something deeper was at play—something beyond individual actions and decisions.

As I dug deep into this, I discovered a powerful yet often invisible force at work: the "Collective Mindset." This shared belief system profoundly influences how groups think, behave, and interact with the world. It can propel a group towards greatness or keep it mired in mediocrity. Unfortunately, many of us are unaware of how much our collective mindsets shape our realities.

I have witnessed how people can perceive wrong as suitable, failure as success, and negativity as positivity simply because their collective mindset has conditioned them to do so. This troubling realisation drove me to write this book— not as an academic exercise but as a call to action. I aim to help others become aware of these hidden forces and shift our collective mindsets towards more productive, sustainable, and empowering directions.

"The Power of a Collective Mindset" is more than a collection of theories; it is a practical guide filled with real-world examples and actionable strategies. Whether you are a leader looking to inspire and unite your team, an entrepreneur aiming to build a cohesive and motivated workforce, or someone seeking to deepen your understanding of human behaviour, this book has something for you.

Inside, you will find:

- **A Deep Understanding of Collective Mindsets**: Learn how shared beliefs shape behaviour and influence outcomes in ways you may not have realised.
- **Tools for Fostering Collaboration**: Discover strategies for creating environments where people naturally align

with your vision, leading to more effective teamwork and innovation.

- **Strategies to Overcome Resistance**: Learn how to build trust and navigate the resistance often accompanying change.
- **Inspiring Global Examples**: Explore case studies from around the world that highlight the transformative power of a unified mindset.

This book is about more than just understanding; it is about transformation. By recognising and reshaping our collective mindsets, we can break free from unproductive patterns and create environments that foster growth, creativity, and lasting success.

I invite you to embark on this journey with me. As you read these pages, reflect on the collective mindsets influencing your life and consider how to apply these lessons to effect positive change. The power to shape our future lies in our ability to harness the collective energy of our communities, organisations, and societies. Together, we can turn challenges into opportunities and potential into reality.

CHAPTER 1

CULTURE

Throughout my life, I have often pondered our society's recurring consequences and conduct. Why do certain cultural norms persist, and why do we rarely question their impact? After much reflection, I realised that the "Collective mindset" lies at the core of all cultural norms. It is the unseen force shaping our actions, beliefs, and culture. This invisible force drives the behaviours we see in organisations, societies, and communities today.

For too long, we have overlooked the profound influence of collective mindsets. They form the bedrock of our "Cultural House," silently orchestrating every positive or negative outcome. The culture we experience in our lives directly manifests the collective mindset we adopt as a group. This unseen force often traces cultural success, stagnation, or failure.

The startling truth is that collective mindsets are pervasive but rarely acknowledged for their role in shaping culture. They are like an undetected virus, quietly influencing every aspect of our society. No societal or organisational culture can thrive without an adaptive and forward-thinking collective mindset.

The Stories of Apple and BlackBerry: A Tale of Two Collective Mindsets

The contrasting stories of Apple and BlackBerry illustrate how a collective mindset can either elevate or undermine a company's success.

Apple's resurgence under Steve Jobs is a testament to the transformative power of a unified, innovation-driven collective mindset. When Jobs returned to Apple in 1997, the company was on the brink of collapse. Its culture was disjointed, and its product line lacked direction. Jobs recognised that to save Apple, he needed to instil a shared mindset of innovation, design excellence, and a relentless focus on user experience.

This mindset was more than just a corporate directive; it became the heartbeat of the entire organisation. Apple was not merely about creating products—it was about developing revolutionary products that would change the world. The iPod, iPhone, and iPad were not just technological feats; they were the physical embodiment of a collective vision that placed the user at the centre of every decision Apple made. This unified culture attracted top talent, fostered customer loyalty, and positioned Apple as a global leader in innovation.

In stark contrast, BlackBerry's decline serves as a cautionary tale about the dangers of neglecting a forward-thinking collective mindset. In the early 2000s, BlackBerry dominated the smartphone market, known for its secure email and physical keyboard. However, as consumer preferences shifted towards larger touchscreens and more user-friendly devices, BlackBerry's leadership clung to their existing product strategy, confident that past success would continue to suffice. This rigid mindset was out of sync with the rapidly evolving market.

BlackBerry's failure to adapt reflected a lack of a forward-looking collective mindset, which ultimately led to the company's rapid decline. While competitors like Apple embraced change and innovation, BlackBerry's internal culture remained stagnant. The absence of a unified, adaptive mindset stifled innovation and crippled their ability to respond to market demands.

Methods for Cultivating a Positive and Productive Culture

The lessons from Apple and BlackBerry underscore the undeniable importance of nurturing a collective mindset to shape a positive culture. Whether in organisations or societies, a unified and adaptive mindset is essential for long-term success. Here are key methods for fostering such a culture:

1. **Define and Communicate Clear Values:** Establishing shared values is crucial for cultivating a unified culture. These values should be consistently communicated across the group and guide decision-making at all levels.

2. **Lead by Example:** Leaders must embody the values and behaviours they wish to see in others. When leaders set strong examples, they inspire others to adopt positive attitudes and practices.

3. **Encourage Open Communication:** A culture of transparency and open dialogue builds trust and ensures issues are addressed before they escalate. Open communication fosters a sense of ownership and collective responsibility.

4. **Promote Collaboration and Teamwork:** Valuing collaboration helps break down silos and encourages the sharing of ideas, fostering innovation and collective problem-solving.

5. **Recognise and Reward Positive Behavior:** Positive reinforcement motivates individuals and reinforces the collective mindset by recognising behaviours aligned with shared values.

6. **Foster Continuous Learning and Development:** A culture that values learning and growth remains dynamic and adaptable. Providing opportunities for continuous education strengthens the collective mindset.

7. **Build a Sense of Community:** Creating a strong community within the group reinforces loyalty and a shared sense of purpose. This sense of belonging is key to fostering long-term commitment to collective values.

8. **Adapt and Evolve:** A positive culture must be adaptable. Regularly assess the group's culture, seek feedback, and be open to change when necessary. Flexibility ensures that the collective mindset remains aligned with the group's goals.

The Power of Moral Leadership in Cultural Transformation

Moral leadership is central to cultural transformation. It is a form of power rooted in ethical principles that guide leaders and organisations towards positive, long-lasting change. A powerful example of moral leadership can be seen in the story of Jackie Robinson, as portrayed in the film *42*.

Branch Rickey, the general manager of the Brooklyn Dodgers, understood that recruiting Jackie Robinson, the first Black player in Major League Baseball, would require more than just physical talent. It required the moral power to withstand immense pressure and racial abuse. When Robinson asked Rickey if he wanted a man with the courage to fight, Rickey responded that he wanted one with the courage not to fight. This was an example of moral power—choosing a higher ethical principle over reactive behaviour.

In the face of adversity, Robinson's calm and principled stance gradually transformed the collective mindset of his teammates. His ability to endure hostility without retaliation sparked sympathy and a cultural shift within the Dodgers. Once resistant, his teammates began to stand by him one by one, leading to a broader cultural transformation within the team and, eventually, the sport.

Moral power goes beyond positional authority or expertise. It is the capacity to inspire change through principled actions that challenge the status quo. This ethical leadership creates a ripple effect, drawing others towards a higher standard and fostering a collective mindset focused on positive change.

The Role of Collective Mindset in Cultural Success

The stories of Apple, BlackBerry, and Jackie Robinson illustrate the undeniable influence of collective mindsets on culture. Whether in business, sports, or society, a group's shared mindset shapes its norms, values, and long-term success. Cultivating a collective mindset that is adaptive, ethical, and focused on shared goals is essential for creating a culture that survives and thrives.

Ignoring the importance of a collective mindset can lead to stagnation and failure, as seen in BlackBerry's decline. On the other hand, consciously fostering a collective mindset aligned with innovation and moral leadership, like at Apple or with Robinson's resilience, paves the way for lasting cultural success.

As we build the cultures within our organisations and societies, we must recognise the power of the collective mindset. By nurturing a unified, adaptable, and ethical perspective, we can create resilient, innovative cultures capable of facing any challenge.

"Collective Mindset is the mother that births our culture" (S. Olamilekan Isreal)

CHAPTER 2

STRUCTURE

often wonder what sets successful people apart from the rest of us. After diving into countless biographies and interviews, one thing keeps popping up: consistency and structure. Those who achieve great things have a knack for sticking to a solid routine.

This realisation has led me to a simple yet powerful conclusion: success thrives on structure, which comes from consistency in our daily actions. As **Aristotle** wisely said, **"We are what we repeatedly do."** Excellence, then, is not an act but a habit. Building a routine is crucial. It helps us map out our day, ensuring we use our time wisely and focus our energy on what truly matters. When we bring structure to our lives, we cultivate a sense of ownership and order that can lead to short and long-term achievements.

Structure is an essential factor that cannot be underestimated when achieving desired results. In the previous chapter, I discussed how the collective mindset is the mother who births every culture. But what about structure? I believe that structure should be considered the genetic framework that births the culture we observe today. This means that the structure we have built also determines the culture we see today. If a structure is a genetic framework that births culture, then the collective mindset is the initial DNA that produces the chromosomes containing many genes. As you change the collective mindset, the genetic framework changes, automatically forming the culture we desire.

As I have grown older, I developed an understanding that each family operates uniquely, following distinct patterns and embracing specific cultures. I realised that these differences stem largely from the family structure. In my own family, I noticed how we had been moulded to follow a particular path that might not mirror the ways of other families. These patterns seem deeply rooted in the structures established by our ancestors, and our parents have chosen to uphold them.

This structure acts as a genetic blueprint, guiding us to adopt a specific way of life and believe, often without question, in its superiority over others.

James Clear's book "Atomic Habits" drives this point home, showing us how small changes can have a significant impact. Improving just one percent daily might not sound like much, but those little steps add up over time. Every considerable achievement starts with a small action. So, why not start small? Build those tiny habits until they become a part of who you are, guiding you towards your goals.

Establishing a routine allows us to prioritise what is essential—taking care of our health, spending time with family, connecting with friends or pushing forward in our careers.

For me, having a good morning routine is highly transformative. Imagine waking up just one hour earlier each day. That hour could be spent meditating, exercising, reading, or enjoying quiet time with yourself. That little slice of "me-time" can work wonders, giving your mind, body, and soul a chance to recharge. It is a moment to think, explore, and grow.

A good routine is, therefore, an investment worth making.

In the corporate world, the importance of structure cannot be overstated. Consider the success of Amazon, a company that embraced a collective mindset and built a robust structure around it. Amazon's structure was designed to foster innovation, efficiency, and customer-centricity. This structure became the genetic framework that shaped Amazon's unique culture, enabling the company to continuously adapt and innovate by streamlining logistics or pioneering cloud computing. Amazon's success story is a testament to how a well-structured framework, grounded in a collective mindset, can lead to extraordinary outcomes. The company's commitment to its core principles of customer obsession, operational excellence, and long-term thinking reflects how structure can powerfully influence culture and results.

On the other hand, let us look at Kodak, a company that once dominated the photography industry but ultimately failed. Kodak's downfall can be traced to its inability to adapt its structure to the digital revolution. Despite having early access to digital photography technology, Kodak's collective mindset remained rooted in the old model of film photography. The company's rigid structure stifled innovation, as decision-makers focused more on protecting their existing business model than embracing the digital future. As a result, Kodak's once-vibrant culture of innovation waned, and the company fell behind its competitors. Kodak's story is a cautionary tale of how ignoring the power of a collective mindset and maintaining a stagnant structure can lead to failure, even for a market leader.

To create structures that support a healthy collective mindset, organisations should:

- Establish a clear vision and values integrated into daily operations and decision-making, ensuring alignment with collective goals.

- Encourage open communication by fostering an environment where feedback is valued and transparency is prioritised, promoting inclusivity and mutual respect.

- Foster collaborative leadership by involving team members in decision-making and empowering them, which enhances buy-in and innovation.

- Create adaptive systems that allow continuous improvement and responsiveness to changing needs, ensuring alignment with current goals.

- Implement continuous learning and development programs that reinforce the collective mindset and keep the organisation dynamic and responsive.

- Align incentives with collective goals by rewarding team achievements and behaviours that reflect the organisation's values, encouraging continued alignment with shared objectives.

- Encourage cross-functional collaboration to break down barriers and bring diverse perspectives together, fostering innovation and a cohesive structure.

- Monitor and reflect on progress regularly to ensure the structure supports the collective mindset, using feedback and performance metrics to refine as needed.

We must consider creating a new framework to achieve different outcomes within families, organisations, and countries. The existing structure reflects our current culture. By expanding our thinking patterns, we can bring about significant change. This is why the collective mindset must not be ignored. As we work to build and refine our structures, we must remember that they are the blueprints for the culture we create.

When aligned with a collective mindset, these structures can lead to a thriving, dynamic environment where success is not only possible but inevitable.

"As we change the "Collective Mindset," the genetic framework changes, automatically forming the culture we desire."
(S. Olamilekan Isreal)

CHAPTER 3

DECISION-MAKING

The reality we live in today is the direct result of our decisions yesterday. Whether these decisions are made individually or collectively, their outcomes are shaped by the mindset that drives them. The quality of our mindset—whether personal or shared within a group—plays a critical role in the effectiveness of our decisions.

When an organisation needs to implement change or address a problem, it typically gathers its executives to deliberate and devise solutions. This scenario underscores the importance of a collective mindset in decision-making. The quality of decisions made by any organisation is inherently tied to the quality of the collective mindset that guides those decisions. A solid collective mindset leads to sound decision-making, while a weak or misaligned mindset can result in poor choices with lasting negative consequences.

This is why many organisations prioritise hiring executives with strong problem-solving and leadership skills. They recognise that the effectiveness of their decision-making process depends on the capabilities and mindset of their leadership team. By ensuring that their leaders have these crucial skills, organisations position themselves to make informed, strategic decisions that drive successful outcomes.

However, decision-making is a double-edged sword—it can be constructive and destructive. Often rooted in a flawed collective mindset, poor decisions can have devastating consequences. I have seen companies make decisions that ultimately led to their downfall. Similarly, nations implement economic policies to spur growth, only to face chaos and decline. In many cases, the adverse outcomes result from the quality—or lack thereof—of the collective mindset within the decision-making team.

For example, consider the contrasting paths taken by Netflix and Motorola, two companies that have faced critical decision points in their histories.

Netflix:

Netflix is a prime example of how a pivotal decision, grounded in a solid collective mindset, can lead to immense success. In the early 2000s, Netflix was primarily a DVD rental service. However, the company's leadership, led by co-founder Reed Hastings, recognised the shifting landscape of technology and media consumption. They understood that the future lay in streaming content directly to consumers, a vision that was not mainstream then.

This decision to pivot from physical DVD rentals to streaming was bold and risky, but it was backed by a collective mindset focused on innovation, adaptability, and anticipating future trends. Netflix invested heavily in technology, content licensing, and original programming, gradually transforming itself into the global streaming giant we know today. The decision saved Netflix from becoming obsolete in a rapidly changing market and positioned it as a leader in the entertainment industry. The collective mindset that embraced change foresaw the future and took calculated risks, which was the key to Netflix's enduring success.

Motorola:

In stark contrast, Motorola's decline is a tale of how poor decision-making, influenced by a misaligned or outdated collective mindset, can lead to disaster. In the 1990s, Motorola was a dominant player in the mobile phone market, renowned for its innovation and technological prowess. However, as the market began to shift towards smartphones, Motorola failed to adapt. The company's leadership held on to its existing product lines and resisted the transition to new technologies, believing its established products would continue to sustain its market position.

This reluctance to embrace change and innovate was rooted in a collective mindset that was overly confident in past successes and resistant to new ideas. As a result, Motorola was quickly outpaced by competitors like Apple and Samsung, who were more attuned to market demands and technological advancements. Motorola's failure to make the necessary strategic decisions at a critical time ultimately led to its downfall, as the company struggled to remain relevant in an industry it once dominated.

Benjamin Franklin once shared his decision-making process in a letter to Joseph Priestley, who sought his advice on a challenging dilemma. Franklin's approach boils down to a simple yet effective method: listing the pros and cons, reflecting on them, and then making a choice. He referred to this as "Prudential Algebra," where each item on the list receives a numerical weight, allowing him to balance out the options. As he put it, **"If I find a Reason pro equal to some two Reasons con, I strike out the three . . . and thus proceeding I find at length where the Ballance lies."**

We often say we "chose" significant life events—like getting married, having children, or starting a new career—but how do we arrive at those choices? Ironically, our most significant decisions sometimes feel less calculated than our smallest ones. We might spend hours debating what to watch on Netflix, only to let a TV show inspire a life-altering move to Paris. Buying a new pair of shoes could take weeks of research, and deciding to end a relationship might happen over a few drinks. In some ways, we are not much different from the ancient Persians, who, according to Herodotus, made important decisions by discussing them sober and then again while drunk.

Reflecting on high-stakes decisions, like President Barack Obama's decision to authorise the raid on Osama bin Laden, we see how those in charge often rely on insights from "decision science," a field that blends behavioural economics, psychology, and management. This strategy can be applied in our own lives.

Take for instance, March 2009, just months into Obama's presidency, when the economy plummeted. Unemployment soared to over eight percent, leading to devastating job losses and financial insecurity for countless families. He opted for the least harmful of three bad options to stabilise the financial system: putting the 19 largest banks through "Stress Tests" to determine their resilience in a worsening economy.

No one was thrilled—indeed, not the public, Wall Street, or even Obama himself. His advisors were divided; some wanted to condemn the reckless bankers, while others worried that would undermine the market confidence they desperately needed.

Obama convened a long meeting with his economic advisors to align his team, listening intently as Treasury Secretary Tim Geithner updated them on the stress tests. They explored various alternatives and pushed each idea to its logical conclusion. By the end of a gruelling day, he left for dinner and a haircut, expecting a consensus upon his return. Yet, during that exhausting process, he had already decided that the stress tests would proceed. Within six months, the economy began to recover, and by the following year, the central banks had repaid every dollar of taxpayer money—plus interest.

The takeaway? Obama understood that tough decisions often come down to probabilities, not certainties, which can burden anyone with the desire for a perfect answer. Rather than getting paralysed by the quest for the ideal solution or following his instincts, he established a sound decision-making framework. He listened to experts, considered the facts, weighed his goals against his principles, and committed to doing his best with the information.

While I have never faced a decision as monumental as launching a covert raid, I have certainly made my share of tough business choices. After all, business is all about decisions.

Some business decisions to be put into thorough consideration are:

- Who to hire?
- Where to invest?
- Should we diversify?
- What inventory do we need to purchase?
- How to engage our employees?
- Navigating financial decisions and more.

In "War and Peace," Tolstoy writes that while an armchair general might imagine himself analysing a campaign on a map, a real general is always caught in the middle of ongoing events, each a link in an endless chain of choices. "Can it be that I allowed Napoleon to get as far as Moscow?" General Kutuzov muses. "When was it decided? Was it yesterday when I sent Platov the order to retreat or the evening before when I dozed off and told Bennigsen to give the orders? Or even earlier?

Unlike the fall of Moscow, the birth of my son was a joyous occasion, yet like Kutuzov, I struggle to pinpoint exactly when I made that epoch-defining choice. It feels monumental, yet the exact moment of its making eludes me, a shared human experience."

Cultivating a Positive and Productive Decision-Making Culture

The stories of Netflix and Motorola highlight the crucial role that a collective mindset plays in decision-making. For any organisation or society aiming to make decisions that will yield positive outcomes, it is essential to cultivate a positive and productive decision-making culture. Here are some methods to achieve this:

1. **Foster a Culture of Innovation:** Encourage continuous learning and experimentation. Organisations should create environments where new ideas are welcomed and calculated risks are supported. This mindset fosters innovation and allows the organisation to adapt to changing circumstances.

2. **Promote Open Communication:** Decision-making should be a collaborative process that values input from diverse

perspectives. Open communication lines ensure that all voices are heard and that decisions are well-rounded and inclusive.

3. **Develop Problem-Solving Skills:** Invest in training programs that enhance problem-solving and critical-thinking skills among team members. A culture that prioritises these skills is better equipped to make informed and effective decisions.

4. **Align Decisions with Long-Term Goals:** Ensure that every decision made aligns with the organisation's long-term vision and goals. Short-term gains should not come at the expense of long-term sustainability.

5. **Encourage Flexibility and Adaptability:** In a rapidly changing world, the ability to pivot and adapt is crucial. Organisations should cultivate a mindset that is open to change and willing to reevaluate strategies as needed.

6. **Empower Decision-Makers:** Ensure that the individuals responsible for making decisions are equipped with the necessary resources, information, and authority. Empowered decision-makers are more confident and effective in their roles.

7. **Evaluate and Learn from Past Decisions:** Regularly review past decisions to assess their outcomes and learn from any mistakes. This reflective practice helps refine the decision-

making process and strengthens the collective mindset over time.

These examples illustrate a collective mindset's profound impact on decision-making within any organisation or society. The quality of decisions is inherently linked to the mindset that underpins them. By nurturing a positive and productive decision-making culture, we create environments where sound, strategic choices that pave the way for sustainable success are made. The contrasting outcomes of Netflix and Motorola vividly demonstrate how the right collective mindset can decide between triumph and failure.

For Tolstoy, the tendency to make tough decisions was one of the great mysteries of existence. It suggested that our life stories are inadequate for their accurate convolution.

"A collective mindset is a powerful force— capable of creating extraordinary success or driving devastating failure."
(S. Olamilekan Isreal)

CHAPTER 4

ADAPTATION

Golly, a nickname given to him by his comrades at the Defense Academy, was known for his imposing physical presence. After winning the national sword championship, he became a major celebrity and often paraded around with an Aide de Camp. The military hierarchy did not mind, as they found him helpful for intimidating hostile nations. However, despite his fearsome reputation, Golly relied mainly on brute strength and lacked sharpness upstairs. He was vulnerable to anyone with enough courage and intelligence. This became evident when a 16-year-old shepherd boy named David, who was underrated, managed to outsmart him.

David knew he could not defeat Golly in close combat due to the latter's strength and size. So, he changed the rules of engagement and opted for a remote combat strategy, selecting five smooth stones and a catapult as his weapons. He calculated the speed of the stone leaving the catapult to be $v = 5$ m/s. Golly, clunky and encumbered by heavy armour, had slow reactions due to his size and high centre of gravity. His lack of flexibility and insistence on close combat played into David's advantage.

The story illustrates the importance of flexibility in life. Change is constant, and inflexibility can lead to negative consequences, whether in marriage, business, or even religion. Adapting to demographic, cultural, and technological shifts is crucial, and rigidity can lead to failure.

Remember, the only constant is change. And oh, David killed Goliath!

Adaptation is fundamental to survival and success in the animal kingdom and within human societies. Just as animals adapt to their environments to thrive—fish to water, lions to land—humans and their collective groups adapt to societal conditions, which shape their paths forward. A lion's dominance of land directly results from its adaptation to that environment; asking it to rule underwater would be absurd. Similarly, the success or failure of human societies is deeply tied to their ability to adapt to changing circumstances.

However, humans possess a unique advantage over animals in terms of adaptation. While animals instinctively adjust to their environments without conscious thought, they cannot change the fundamental aspects of their nature. For example, a lion cannot decide to start eating fruit instead of flesh; its biological instincts bind it. On the other hand, humans have been endowed with the remarkable ability to choose and change what they adapt to consciously. This capacity, granted by a higher power, sets us apart and enables us to shape our destiny in ways that animals cannot.

Consider how humans can decide to alter their diets, becoming vegetarians or vegans by choice, or how they can transform their lifestyles, shifting from passive to active. Similarly, societies and organisations can change long-standing practices and norms in response to new realities. This ability to choose our adaptation is rooted in our mindset. The collective mindset of a group—whether it be a family, community, company, or an entire nation—determines what that group will adapt to and how it will respond to challenges and opportunities.

Take India, for example. For decades, the country was characterised by slow economic growth, often called the "Hindu growth rate." This period marked protectionist policies, heavy regulation, and a general acceptance of the status quo. The collective mindset was one of limited ambition and acceptance of modest growth. However, this began to change in the early 1990s when India underwent significant economic reforms. The government, driven by a new collective mindset, started embracing liberalisation, privatisation, and globalisation. This shift in perspective and policy led to an economic transformation that saw India emerge as one of the fastest-growing major economies in the world.

India's collective mindset transitioned from cautious stagnation to dynamic growth, driven by the belief that the nation could compete on a global scale. This new mindset encouraged innovation, entrepreneurship, and investment, propelling the country to remarkable economic heights over the last two decades. India's story is a testament to how a collective shift in mindset and strategic adaptation can lead to extraordinary outcomes.

On the other hand, we can look at countries that have failed to adapt their collective mindset to changing global dynamics, resulting in prolonged periods of economic and social stagnation. One such example is Zimbabwe. Zimbabwe was known as the "Breadbasket of Africa" for years due to its robust agricultural sector. However, poor policy decisions, a lack of adaptability, and an entrenched collective mindset that resisted change led to economic collapse and widespread poverty. The country's failure to adapt to new economic realities and its persistence in outdated practices have been cemented in difficulties, preventing it from realising its potential.

These examples illustrate the critical role that a collective mindset plays in a society's ability to adapt and thrive. Adaptability is not just about responding to change; it is about proactively shaping one's future in the face of inevitable challenges. A resilient collective mindset embraces change, fosters innovation, and remains open to new possibilities.

Webster's Dictionary defines adaptable as "Able to change or be changed to fit or work better in some situation or for some purpose."

Most employers look for this skill when recruiting. They look for people who are flexible and able to adapt to changes in their workstations, either physically or in terms of work expectations. Many people are chronic, and when presented with a storyline that requires them to change their usual way of doing things, they feel threatened, agitated, and unwilling to flow with the new changes.

Often, things do not go how you plan or want them. You might have planned to land a good job right out of college so you can buy a car and live a comfortable life. What happens when this does not occur as planned? Do you fold your hands and dwell in self-pity, or do you morph to make meaning of whatever curveball life has thrown you?

Adaptability is a crucial skill for entrepreneurs in the 21st century, as they face unprecedented challenges and opportunities in a rapidly evolving world.

Adaptability is considered a vital leadership skill. However, much like emotional and cultural intelligence, adaptability as a leadership skill has not received the attention it deserves. Numerous leaders have adapted to new technology, market trends, the fast-paced and evolving tech industry, and the need for continuous improvement. Jeff Bezos, Sheryl Sandberg, Steve Jobs, and Mark Zuckerberg are famous leaders who have embraced adaptability. However, it is unnecessary to be in the C-suite (or with a title as CEO or COO) to have any leadership skills, let alone adaptability. We must motivate and encourage our teams to adapt to changing environments.

> *"The greatest glory in living lies not in never falling, but in rising every time we fall."*
> *(Nelson Mandela)*

The above quote speaks to both adaptability and resilience. It emphasises the importance of picking yourself up after experiencing setbacks or failures and moving forward despite the challenges that may come your way.

Nelson Mandela learnt to adapt to vastly different environments, from the tribal villages of his youth to the brutal confines of Robben Island. In business, adapting to change is crucial for survival and growth.

Importance of Adaptability in Maintaining a Resilient Collective Mindset

Adaptability is the cornerstone of resilience. It allows a society or organisation to weather storms, pivot in response to new challenges, and grow despite adversity. A collective mindset that values adaptability is essential for sustaining long-term success. When flexible and open to new ideas, groups are better equipped to handle disruptions and turn potential threats into opportunities.

This is where the power of human choice comes into play. Unlike animals, who cannot alter their fundamental behaviours, humans can choose to change the conditions they adapt to. Many societal norms and practices are accepted as unchangeable simply because they have been ingrained in us for so long. We raise our children to accept these conditions, perpetuating cycles of stagnation and limiting our collective potential. However, by recognising that our adaptation results from our collective mindset, we can begin to think outside the box and challenge the status quo. To change what we adapt to, we must first change our perspective.

Enhancing adaptability within a collective mindset can be achieved by fostering continuous learning, engaging in scenario planning, promoting cross-cultural collaboration, and establishing feedback mechanisms. Developing adaptive and forward-thinking leaders is crucial for setting a tone of flexibility and responsiveness throughout the group.

Adaptation is a survival mechanism and a pathway to growth and success. The collective mindset of a group, organisation, or nation is the driving force behind its ability to adapt. We can build resilient cultures that thrive in an ever-changing world by fostering a mindset that embraces change, values continuous learning, and remains flexible in the face of new challenges. The stories of India and Zimbabwe highlight the importance of adaptability in determining whether a society prospers or falls behind. Let us, therefore, commit to nurturing a collective mindset that is open to change, poised for growth, and ready to turn challenges into opportunities.

"The greatest glory in living lies not in never falling, but in rising every time we fall."
(Nelson Mandela)

CHAPTER 5

BELIEF & SPIRITUALITY

While growing up, I used to believe that God would take care of everything for me and that the laws of cause and effect were just technicalities. Like many in my generation, I thought I was overlooking what truly mattered and questioned why certain practices were ingrained in our lives. Whenever I asked about these traditions, my mother would respond with the same explanations, rooted in beliefs passed down through generations. I cannot blame her; like so many others, she followed a pattern handed down by those before her, hoping for a different outcome. But this is the crux of ignorance—"TO-IGNORE-IMPORTANCE."

My awakening came when I encountered a powerful verse in 1 Corinthians 13:11, where Paul says, *"When I was a child, I spoke as a child, I understood as a child, I thought as a child: but when I became a man, I put away childish things."* This scripture struck a chord, making me realise I was not alone in childish thinking. Ignorance, as I have come to understand it, is not just a lack of knowledge; it is a failure to challenge our inherited beliefs to analyse the patterns we follow unthinkingly. The collective mindset, shaped by years of unexamined assumptions, is the root of our current realities. We have inherited patterns from our ancestors, and without challenging them, we continue to see the same outcomes, generation after generation.

I believe that ignorance plays a significant role in why we often cling to the beliefs of our predecessors. While ignorance contributes to this, the actual driver behind the outcomes we see today is the power of a collective mindset. We have become entrenched in patterns passed down through generations, leading us to experience the same results repeatedly. Expecting change without challenging these inherited beliefs is a flawed approach. I have questioned many of these entrenched ideas throughout my life, leading some of my family, friends, and colleagues to label me as conventional. However, I do not fault them, as our perspectives differ. I am reminded of a quote from one of my mentors, **Bishop David Oyedepo**: **"Life is in phases, and men are in sizes."**

Similarly, **Mother Teresa** wisely said, **"You can do what I cannot do. I can do what you cannot do. Together, we can**

do great things." These quotes have deeply resonated with me over the years. They highlight that while others may not share my views, it does not mean they lack understanding; instead, their beliefs shape them differently. Through my interactions with them, I have always gleaned valuable insights.

India and Nigeria are countries where the collective mindset is deeply intertwined with spiritual beliefs. These nations hold firm to their spiritual traditions, often placing faith in mysticism and the power of prayer to solve their problems. Yet, despite being among the most spiritually devout countries in the world, they grapple with some of the most challenging economic conditions. This begs the question: Can a nation pray for its way to prosperity? The evidence suggests otherwise. Spirituality and prayer, while powerful, must be balanced with practical actions and strategies. Without this balance, spirituality alone cannot fuel economic growth or solve systemic issues.

I recall a thought-provoking story shared by my good friend, Mr. Gbolagade. He told me about a Nigerian pastor who travelled some years ago to one of the Scandinavian countries, likely Norway. During one of his beach outings, the pastor initiated a conversation with an elderly lady, attempting to share the message of Jesus with her.

The woman asked, "What country are you from?"

"Nigeria," he replied.

"Oh, I see," she responded. "Yes, you folks over there do need Jesus. But here, we don't. Our hospitals, government, and police work just fine."

At first glance, her remark stung, but she had a point. Many prayer points in Nigeria revolve around healthcare, governance, and security. However, in places like Norway, Sweden, and Denmark, these aspects of life function efficiently, reducing the need for divine intervention in everyday matters.

What does this story teach us? It highlights that while prayer and fasting are essential, some breakthroughs require more than spiritual effort—they demand a change in mindset and action. Countries like Denmark did not abandon faith; they prioritised working towards innovation and systems that function. They achieved collective progress by focusing on practical solutions and adopting an innovative mindset. Today, Denmark's success is not the result of endless prayers but of a collective mindset that values action alongside faith.

This story reminds us that while spiritual growth is essential, true transformation happens when combined with hard work, creativity, and strategic thinking.

On the other hand, consider China—a country where spirituality is also significant but where the collective mindset embraces the law of cause and effect. The Chinese people understand that while spirituality and belief systems are essential, they must be accompanied by hard work, strategic planning, and disciplined execution. China's economic rise is a testament to a collective mindset that values spirituality and the practical application of the law of cause and effect. Their success is not the result of prayers alone but a balanced approach where spiritual beliefs coexist with a strong work ethic and a commitment to progress.

The role of belief and spirituality in shaping societies is profound. Spiritual beliefs can be a powerful, unifying force, bringing people together under a shared vision. Yet, they can also be divisive, especially when different groups cling to conflicting interpretations of spirituality. Throughout history, spiritual communities with strong collective mindsets have achieved remarkable feats driven by a shared belief system that empowers them to overcome challenges. For example, the early Christian communities, despite persecution, thrived and grew because of their unwavering collective belief in their faith.

Much research over the past ten years has proven that spiritual people flourish faster. Spirituality is linked to many vital aspects of human behaviour; spiritual people have positive relationships, higher self-esteem, are more optimistic, and follow an essential purpose in life. Psychology has demonstrated that expressing gratitude for what we have is associated with many positive emotions, such as optimism, generosity with time and resources, and overall vitality. When we walk our talk through our actions and behaviour as a spiritual person, we affirm these vital emotions correspond to being truly successful.

Sometimes ago, I listened to a short reflection about how small actions can make a big difference. The example used was how significant it was for Desmond Tutu when, as a young boy, he saw a white priest doff his hat in courtesy to his mother, who was a domestic worker. Growing up under apartheid in South Africa, he had never seen a white man show such respect to a black person before, and it had a profound impact on him.

Tutu later learnt that the priest he had met as a young boy was the great anti-apartheid campaigner Trevor Huddleston. Among all the "important" things that Huddleston achieved in his life, he would never have imagined this simple act of courtesy's impact. Yet Tutu cited it as a critical moment in his upbringing, a moment that helped set him on the incredible path he took to help bring hope and change to millions of people.

The story of how Huddleston's small act made such a big difference got me thinking about the areas of life that should be affected by our faith. In what ways should faith make a difference in how we live?

These are the ones I came up with:

- Privately, authentic faith should constantly change us in ways we only know about. Through prayer, we seek God's grace to shape and influence our inner lives, to allow divine love to repair, restore, and re-orientate us. Genuine faith makes a difference when no one is watching.

- Personally, authentic faith influences our small, daily decisions about how we behave, like our attitude when driving and how we treat our families. But it also influences the big choices that we make about our lives: the house we buy, how we use our money, and where we send our children to school. Faith is expressed in the personal values we live by.

- Practically, authentic faith is expressed in actions that make it tangible and visible to others, especially those who are poor and suffering. Beliefs only become faith when they are put into action. The Bible continually emphasises the inseparability of loving God and loving our neighbours. God blesses us and allows us to be a blessing to others.

- Professionally, authentic faith has to be expressed in the realms where we spend most of our time and energy—and for many of us, that is paid employment. There is no sacred or secular divide in reality: the workplace is as significant a realm as the "church" for expressing our faith and hope in the living God.

- Publicly, authentic faith can never accept being relegated to a private realm. Faith has things to say about how society is ordered and how communities operate. From the start, Christianity was a public movement, described in the New Testament as the "Ekklesia," which means public assembly. Back then, the Christian faith was never seen as a "private matter," and neither is it today.

- Politically, authentic faith cares about how the structures and powers in the world can be shaped to create greater fairness, justice, and peace. When we look at the injustices and violence in places such as Iraq, Syria, and Gaza, we cannot pretend that faith has nothing to do with politics. If Jesus had not been a political threat to the Jewish and Roman authorities, then he never would have been crucified.

Of course, this is far easier to write than live out. And, of course, different branches of the Church have different strengths regarding these areas. This is why unity among Christians is essential, so we have to work together to show the difference that faith makes. Faith must make a difference in how we live. As Brennan Manning wrote:

> "The greatest cause of atheism is Christians who acknowledge Jesus with their lips, then walk out the door and deny him with their lifestyle. That is what an unbelieving world finds unbelievable."

However, spiritual beliefs can also lead to division when they become rigid or exclusionary. Sometimes, communities or nations have been torn apart because differing spiritual beliefs fostered intolerance and conflict. The key to harnessing spirituality's power positively lies in promoting an open, inclusive, and balanced collective mindset. Spirituality should inspire unity, drive positive actions, and support practical efforts towards growth and development.

To foster strong, positive beliefs within a group, it is essential to encourage a culture of continuous questioning and learning. Spirituality should not be about blind adherence to traditions. It should be about seeking a more profound understanding and applying it to enhance collective well-being. Leaders within spiritual communities must emphasise the importance of balancing belief with action, ensuring that spiritual practices contribute to tangible outcomes that benefit the group.

My faith has always been central to me. I am not a cultural Christian.

For me, faith is not a surface reality or a Sunday ritual. I do not know God religiously. Some people fall out of faith because they do not know God; they know about God. They hope to please God through tedious ritualistic simulations of piety—fasting, vigil, program attendance and works.

God introduced himself to me through his intellect. I picked up the Bible and saw the Holy Spirit's intellectual sagacity, insight, linguistic prowess, and brilliant grammatical construct.

I could not get over the logical reasoning in Paul's letters. As an engineering student, I found it enthralling.

I was soon introduced to phenomena. On Monday, outside the church, I began to see the supernatural. I started to experience the spatiotemporal continuum. Intellect became fun. My processing speed became phenomenal. I began to demonstrate the unimaginable in the field of knowledge. Forgive me if this sounds like a gasconade. I am just trying to introduce a dimension of God to you.

Do not be fooled by my jeans, designer shoes, funky t-shirts, and beautiful wife. Behind all this is spiritual solidity. God powers the endless stream of creative intelligence you see.

Despite my busyness, I devote time and energy to these blogs because I want to make introductions. I want you to meet "Jesus the Logos" to explore God's rational, creative, and intellectual dimensions. It is an adventure.

One cannot help but wonder: where are the visionary leaders of our time? A question Nebuchadnezzar might have pondered, he understood nations and economies are built with intellectual assets. His program of assimilation was predicated on that insight. Daniel and Co. were on that program. He went for the best brains.

Pharaoh Sesostris knew that, too. He saw brilliance in Joseph and quickly amended Egypt's constitution. Joseph had analytical ability and proffered practical, measurable solutions.

Every CEO is looking for Daniel and Joseph. CEOs are not looking for prayer warriors and night vigil legionnaires.

We need to stop this frontloading of religion; this exhibitionist takes pride in fasting, night vigils, stickers, and conventions. Daniel prayed out of view. Doubtfully, he wore a "Repent and Be Saved" badge to work or carried a Bible the size of Noah's ark. It does not prove anything. Enough of "Rigidity in Christianity." The lunch hour fellowship? Why, really? It satisfies the religious spirit but is of doubtful efficacy. Eat your lunch and rest. It would be best if you had both for performance.

Dressing like a member of the Amish sect does not show that you are a Christian. It is not holiness, just retrogressive fashion sense. You limit your corporate advancement with all these impertinent symbolic externalisations.

Dress sharp, be sharp on your feet, and be sharp in your spirit. Consult on your knees, away from view. Spirituality is supposed to look normal, not dramatised. In Him (Christ), you live, move, and have your being—a normalised existence.

You cannot go for night vigil and sleep at work. You are robbing Peter. If you are spiritual, let it show in your productivity. Let us see it in your output if you claim to know God. The people will discern God is with you from your performance.

You cannot claim to be spiritual and also be sleeping in class. That is a lack of focus. Cut out all those extracurricular spiritual programs and concentrate on your studies. It is why you are in school. Brilliance is spirituality. That is the Logos dimension.

My mission is to foster a thoughtful and vibrant faith.

I believe sermons should be subjected to Berean rigour, questions asked, and intelligent answers provided. I think that people should be taught theology, not just situational gospel.

We can access God's incredible mind for strategic, business, and professional challenges. God is God on Sunday, but he is also God on Monday. He is God in church, and he is God outside church. God is limitless.

Christians should be versatile in knowledge and widely read in philosophy, sociology, government, IT, economics, literature, comparative religious studies, and science. Paul showed us that intellect is a tool of faith.

I believe excellence should be a motto of faith. Daniel and Co. are profiled in the Bible to serve as typologies, role models, and inspirations for youths. Daniel had a spirit of excellence.

I believe science is not anti-faith and that God created science. Genesis can be resolved scientifically, and the prevailing Gap Theory in Christian theology has too many gaps. A new model is required.

I believe the gifts of the spirit are not limited in scope to the church; in particular, the intelligence group of those gifts—

word of wisdom, word of knowledge, and prophecy—have secular capacities.

In pursuing intelligent faith, I concluded that the "seed principle" preached in the church is a retail prosperity principle. At optimum efficiency, it can only deliver 25% congregational productivity—Jesus said so. It cannot answer the question of mass poverty in my country. The right tool is policy. Christians must get involved in politics and governance, if only for the sake of the people. Not participating in the political process is a faith malpractice bordering on recklessness.

Belief and spirituality are powerful forces that shape the collective mindset of any group, society, or nation. They have the potential to unite or divide, to inspire greatness, or to maintain the status quo. The difference between a society that thrives and one that stagnates often lies in how well it balances its spiritual beliefs with practical actions. By cultivating a collective mindset that values both spirituality and the law of cause and effect, we can create environments where spiritual practices contribute to real, lasting progress.

"Ignorance isn't just a lack of knowledge; it's a failure to challenge the beliefs we've inherited, to scrutinise the patterns we follow blindly." (S. Olamilekan Isreal)

CHAPTER 6

INNOVATION

Have you ever wondered why certain societies stand out for innovation and creativity? The key lies in the environment individuals are exposed to, their upbringing, and how they think. These factors form a collective mindset, which is pivotal in shaping a society's approach to creativity and innovation. If we aspire for our children to grow as creative individuals, we must nurture creativity in our approach and expose them to a rich array of cognitive resources.

As a child, my mind was always buzzing with creative thoughts. I constantly asked questions, challenged norms, and thought outside the box. Yet, I was raised in a conventional family, which often led to confusion. My mother, deeply rooted in tradition, contrasted sharply with my father, a well-traveled businessman with an open-minded approach. This clash of parenting styles left me uncertain about whether to embrace my creative side fully.

This lack of a solid collective mindset during my formative years hindered my ability to embrace creativity. It took me a long time to realise that one of my purposes in life is to create things that benefit others and solve real-world problems. Even after this realisation, I struggled to bring my ideas to life due to the absence of a supportive collective mindset that encouraged innovation.

Years later, new experiences, global travel, and exposure to self-development resources reignited my creative spark. I began to see the world through a different lens, finding a community that nurtured and encouraged my creativity. This support allowed me to create resources aimed at improving lives and helping others. I hope my journey will resonate with readers and inspire them to find value in their creativity.

I am reminded of a poignant quote by **Nnamdi Azikiwe:** **"Give me my youth back, and I will pay any price for it."** This sentiment has always resonated with me, often making me wish to turn back time and redefine my journey. Had I grown up with parents who valued creativity, I might have authored numerous books, made a more meaningful impact on society, and been even more influential than I am today. However, without my upbringing, how would I have recognised the value of creativity or understood the importance of fostering a collective mindset in parenting? How would I be able to guide my children towards embracing creativity today?

As I write this book today, my eight-year-old daughter demonstrates creative thinking and innovation, eagerly presenting her creations to our family. I am filled with immense joy witnessing her unbridled creativity, which reminds me of the importance of nurturing this trait from a young age.

Innovation often involves transforming creative ideas into new solutions that drive business growth, improve efficiency, and meet customers' changing needs while enhancing decision-making and problem-solving across the organisation.

Think about Tesla's commitment to putting the first electric vehicle on the road in 2008 or Google's introduction of a search engine in 1998. Each innovation was unheard of at the time and represented a significant paradigm shift.

Even if modern businesses do not innovate at this same level, innovation is still crucial today. Not only does it offer the potential for increased profit, but it can also create new jobs and increase customer trust.

The narrative of innovation, often dominated by familiar figures, overlooks the diverse array of minds that have shaped our world. Among these is Marie Van Brittan Brown, an African

American woman whose pioneering invention emerged from the necessity of ensuring her family's safety in Queens during the 1960s. Her story is a testament to the power of the innovation mindset, .which can serve as a profound catalyst for change regardless of one's background.

Brown's legacy offers a critical lesson in innovation. It recognises the importance of identifying and harnessing creativity to meet a need. Brown, working as a nurse, needed a way to feel safe when she was home alone. She devised the first modern home security system, which required ingenuity and perseverance against the odds.

Brown's journey to innovation was not straightforward. The development of her security system, which included a camera, a two-way microphone, and remote door locking, encountered the typical hurdles of funding and familiarity with the patent process. Yet, she persisted, her dedication eventually culminating in a patent in 1969. This achievement, however, was only part of the journey.

Her invention laid the groundwork for a sector now valued in the billions, proving that the seeds of significant change can sprout from the most personal concerns. It was an innovation born out of the immediate need for safety and the foresight to create a system that could one day be used by millions.

Brown's story is especially significant because it challenges the prevailing perceptions of who can be an innovator. It reinforces the message that the ability to innovate is not the province of a select few but a potential harboured in all, waiting to be ignited by circumstance and nurtured through effort and resilience.

The Role of Innovation in Shaping Nations

Remember the Kodak company? In 1997, Kodak had about 160,000 employees, and about 85% of the world's photography was done with Kodak cameras. With the rise of mobile cameras over the past few years, Kodak Camera Company is out of the market. Even Kodak went completely bankrupt, and all his employees were fired.

At the same time, many more famous companies had to stop themselves. Like:

- HMT (clock)
- BAJAJ (bike)
- DYANORA (TV)
- MURPHY (radio)
- NOKIA (mobile)
- RAJDOOT (bike)
- AMBASSADOR (car)

None of the these companies had bad quality. Why are these companies lowly regarded in the current age? Because they could not change themselves over time.

Standing in the present moment, you probably do not think how much the world could change in the next ten years! Today's 70%-90% jobs will be completely gone in the next ten years. We are slowly entering the era of the "Fourth Industrial Revolution."

Check out today's famous companies.

UBER is just a software name. No, they have no cars of their own. Yet today, the world's largest taxi-fair company is UBER.

Airbnb is the largest hotel company in the world today. But the funny thing is they do not own a single hotel in the world.

There is no work for new lawyers in America today because a legal software called IBM Watson can advocate much better than any new lawyer. Thus, almost 90% of Americans will not have jobs in the next ten years. The remaining ten percent will be saved. These ten percent will be known as the experts.

The new doctor is also sitting down to work. Watson software can detect cancer and other diseases four times more accurately than humans. Computer intelligence will surpass human intelligence by 2030.

90% of today's cars will not be seen on the roads in the next 20 years. Leftover cars will either run on electricity or hybrid vehicles. The roads will slowly become empty. Gasoline consumption will decrease, and oil-producing Arab countries will slowly become bankrupt.

If you want a car you have to ask for a car from a software like Uber. And as soon as you ask for a car, a completely driverless car will come and park in front of your door. If you travel with several people in the same car, the rent of a car per person will be less than a bike.

Driving without a driver will reduce the number of accidents by 99%. And this is why car insurance will stop, and car insurance companies will be out.

Things like driving on earth will no longer survive. Traffic police and parking staff will not be required when 90% of vehicles disappear from the road.

Just think, there used to be STD booths in the streets even ten years ago. All these STD booths were forced to close after the mobile revolution came into the country. Those who survived have become mobile recharge shops. Again, there is an online revolution in mobile recharge. People started recharging their mobile online sitting at home. They had to replace these recharge shops again. Now, these are just mobile phones to buy and sell and repair shops. But this will also change very soon. Mobile phone sales are increasing directly from Amazon and Flipkart.

The definition of money is also changing. There used to be cash, but in today's age, it has become "plastic money." The credit card and debit card round was a few days ago. Now that too is changing, and the era of mobile wallets is coming—the growing market of Paytm, one click of mobile money.

Those who cannot change with age are removed from the earth. So, keep changing with the times.

When we look at the world, it becomes evident that some countries are celebrated for their innovative prowess while others lag far behind. Nations like Japan, China, South Korea, and the USA have become synonymous with innovation. Their societies have cultivated a collective mindset that values creativity, risk-taking, and continuous improvement. This mindset is reflected in their economies, which are some of the most dynamic and forward-thinking in the world.

Japan, with its culture of precision and continuous improvement, has given rise to groundbreaking technologies and products that have revolutionised industries. China, combining spiritual beliefs with a strong emphasis on the law of cause and effect, has rapidly transformed itself into a global economic powerhouse. South Korea, once a war-torn nation, has become a leader in technology and pop culture through relentless innovation. The USA, with its culture of entrepreneurship and freedom of thought, continues to be a hub of creativity, driving global trends in technology, entertainment, and business.

In stark contrast, countries like Niger, Angola, and Burundi struggle with innovation. Their societies often lack the creative mindset necessary to foster growth and development. The absence of a supportive environment for creativity has left these nations trailing behind, unable to keep pace with the rapidly changing world. Their economies remain stagnant, and they struggle to provide opportunities for their citizens to thrive.

The Purpose of Innovation and How Collective Mindset Shapes Its Meaning in Our Society

I recently came across a post where someone mentioned in an interview that AI was designed to "ruin our minds." But how could that be? This perspective highlights the importance of being mindful of the leaders we follow and the collective beliefs we adopt as a society. Like many other innovations, AI was created to enhance efficiency, boost productivity, and improve our way of life—not to harm it. If we view such technology as a threat, we may miss the actual value of progress and productivity.

Take, for example, a furniture company that recently revolutionised its business with AI. Customers no longer had to spend hours debating which pieces best fit their home. Instead, AI provided instant, personalised recommendations, saving time and transforming the shopping experience into something more enjoyable and productive for everyone involved. This is innovation at its best—working to improve lives.

So, why do some societies view innovation, like AI, as a threat? The answer often lies in their collective mindset. In certain cultures, there is a belief that success can only be achieved through hardship and struggle. The idea that something could make life easier and more efficient is seen not as progress but as a shortcut that undermines the value of hard work. This mindset leads to resistance to change and a fear of the unknown, blocking the very progress that innovation offers.

A society's collective mindset shapes how people view change and innovation. In cultures where the belief that success must come through suffering is ingrained, innovation will always be seen as a threat rather than an opportunity. But innovation is not a threat—it is a powerful tool for unlocking our potential, increasing productivity, and improving the quality of our lives.

We must challenge these limiting beliefs. Rejecting innovations that empower people to work smarter and live more efficiently is shortsighted. True progress comes when we embrace change and the innovations that help us grow as individuals and as a society. Every new idea holds the potential to reshape our future, and the collective mindset we choose will determine whether that future is one of progress or stagnation.

As we navigate the complexities of this digital age, it is essential to remember that AI and other technologies are not replacements for human abilities—they are tools. Rather than fearing being replaced, we must harness the power of technology to amplify our capabilities. Machines may excel at certain tasks but lack the creativity, emotional intelligence, and social acumen that define human strength.

As a life coach, I have seen the transformative impact of embracing technology in the workplace. Instead of succumbing to fear, individuals should focus on upskilling and adapting to this evolving landscape. By fostering a symbiotic relationship between humans and technology, we open the door to unprecedented growth and innovation.

Leadership in the age of AI demands a shift in our collective mindset—one that recognises that "humans rule the world." Rather than viewing technology as a threat, leaders should integrate it into their strategies, enhancing efficiency and allowing human resources to focus on more fulfilling and strategic endeavours.

The future belongs to those who can adapt and thrive alongside the tools that may initially spark fear. When we embrace the synergy between human ingenuity and technological innovation, we unlock a future where both coexist harmoniously, creating limitless opportunities for growth and transformation.

When approached with the right mindset, innovation is not a disruption—it is the key to greater effectiveness, productivity, and fulfilment. We must always ask ourselves how innovation can serve us and drive positive change in our lives and the world around us. This thoughtful, proactive approach ensures that innovation continues to be a force for good, shaping a brighter future for all of society.

The Impact of Collective Mindsets on Innovation

The difference between these countries lies in their collective mindsets. Innovative societies strongly emphasise education, curiosity, and experimentation. These societies understand that failure is not the end but a stepping stone to success. They encourage their citizens to think critically, question the status quo, and explore new ideas. This collective mindset is ingrained in their education systems, workplaces, and communities, creating fertile ground for innovation.

In contrast, societies that are left behind in innovation often have a collective mindset that resists change. They may cling to traditional practices and beliefs, viewing them as sacrosanct, even when they no longer serve their purpose. This resistance to change stifles creativity and discourages individuals from thinking outside the box. Even those with creative potential find it difficult to innovate without a supportive environment.

Nurturing a collective mindset that prioritises creativity, values diversity, and promotes continuous learning is crucial to cultivating a culture of innovation. This can be achieved by fostering critical thinking in education, creating environments that view failure as a learning opportunity, encouraging collaboration across diverse perspectives, and ensuring that leaders model and reward innovative behaviour.

Innovation is not just about coming up with new ideas; it is about creating a collective mindset that supports creativity and continuous improvement. The most innovative societies have cultivated environments where creativity is encouraged and risk-taking is rewarded. By fostering a culture of innovation, we can empower individuals and communities to thrive, driving progress and creating a better future for all.

Reflecting on my journey, I am grateful for the lessons I have learnt and the opportunities I have had to embrace creativity. I hope that by sharing my experiences, I can inspire others to recognise the importance of innovation and nurture a collective mindset that values creativity and continuous learning. Let us build a future where innovation is not just the domain of a few but a shared value that drives us all forward.

"If you're not creative in your thinking, you cannot be creative in real life."
(S. Olamilekan Isreal)

CHAPTER 7

LEADERSHIP

Years ago, I came across a remarkable book on leadership by Stephen Covey titled "The 21 Irrefutable Laws of Leadership." One chapter, "The Law of Empowerment," left a lasting impression on me. Covey shared his experiences with two childhood games: "King of the Hill" and "Follow the Leader." The goal of "King of the Hill" was to knock others down to claim leadership—a striking metaphor for how many leaders operate today, climbing to the top at the expense of others.

Covey also examined the leadership style of Henry Ford, whose habit of undermining his executives ultimately harmed his own company. Whenever an executive became too influential, Ford cut them down by reassigning them to lesser roles, supporting their subordinates, or publicly humiliating them. Ford believed in keeping his people anxious and off-balance, a toxic philosophy that Lee Iacocca, one of Ford's successors, later adopted. Iacocca realised too late that this destructive style was a product of the environment Ford had created. Such leadership does not just shape organisations; it can influence entire societies, embedding a collective mindset that values power and control over empowerment and collaboration.

Reflecting on these ideas, I am reminded of a quote I often share: "Your attitude as a leader shapes the environment around you. Leadership doesn't just influence people; it transforms the whole environment." This speaks to the profound impact leadership has on a collective mindset. We must be discerning about the leaders we choose to follow because leadership is inherently influential—it can either elevate or degrade a society's collective mindset. Influence is, indeed, the father of the "Collective mindset."

A conversation with my editor and a very close friend brought this into even sharper focus. He said, "If a particular group of people are used to abnormality, everything that is normal and impactful becomes abnormal." This statement has stayed with me, leading me to wonder why so many people have been conditioned to accept abnormality and immorality as the norm. It is a disheartening reality and a pervasive problem that has stunted the potential of our youth. I have come to believe that misguided leadership is the root cause.

In my country, the prevailing concept of leadership often mirrors the destructive style exemplified by Henry Ford and, later, Lee Iacocca. This approach, though adequate for those seeking power, has left a profound and lasting negative impact on our collective mindset. It has become so entrenched that people frequently distrust or reject leaders who offer a different, more positive approach.

For many years, I have believed that the best way to become an effective leader is to empower others rather than to seek personal enrichment. Stephen Covey echoed this sentiment: "The only way to make yourself indispensable is to make yourself dispensable." By empowering others to develop the skills and confidence to take over your role, you become invaluable to the organisation. However, this principle may not resonate in societies where the collective mindset is shaped by a different, less empowering leadership style.

One personal experience that remains etched in my memory is when I hired my first HR manager, Precious, during the early days of my leadership as president of my company. I was committed to creating a thriving work environment and empowering my employees. Precious, one of our earliest hires, was entrusted with shaping the company's culture. She and the company would flourish by embracing an empowerment-focused leadership approach.

From the very beginning, I invested heavily in her growth and gave her the autonomy to make decisions that could propel the company forward. However, over time, I noticed something was off. Despite my best efforts and constant support, the HR department was not progressing as I had hoped. Precious seemed disengaged and unresponsive to the empowerment opportunities I offered.

Frustrated by the lack of progress, I addressed the issue head-on. I called a meeting with the executive team and asked Precious for her perspective during the discussion. I wanted to understand what might have gone wrong and how I could better support her. Surprisingly, she could not give a clear answer. It became apparent that Precious had not fully embraced or even appreciated the company culture we were striving to build.

Realising the misalignment, we gave Precious time off to reflect and rebuild herself, hoping she would come back stronger and more aligned with our company's vision. But she has yet to return, and we ultimately had to hire a new HR manager. From the start, we brought in Michael, who demonstrated the adaptability and commitment needed to drive our culture forward.

This experience taught me a powerful lesson. Precious' resistance was not a failure of leadership on my part but rather a reflection of a mindset that did not align with the leadership culture we were creating. She had been conditioned to expect a different leadership style—perhaps more directive or hands-on—and could not adapt to our empowerment-focused approach. This experience reinforced for me the importance of hiring individuals who possess the right skills and mindset to grow with the organisation's vision. It was a reminder that leadership is not just about empowering others but ensuring that those we empower are ready to embrace that responsibility.

We must demonstrate ethical and empowering leadership to raise moral and empowered youth. Leadership is an influential force that shapes societies, guiding their thoughts, behaviours, and, ultimately, their collective mindset. When done right, leadership has the power to mould individuals for years, often without their conscious awareness. The only way to counteract negative leadership is to gradually distance ourselves from leaders who propagate harmful mindsets. Negative leadership creates a collective mindset that permeates societies over time. The saying goes, "As we lay our bed, so we must lie on it." The leadership mindset we project into the world shapes our society into what we see today.

In 2009, Time magazine asked Katsuaki Watanabe why Toyota was more profitable than America's top three car manufacturers combined. Watanabe responded that, at Toyota, everyone works as a team. Toyota even sees its suppliers as partners. This is not an isolated case. There is increasing evidence that shared leadership, better teamwork, and collaboration with stakeholders can make a big difference in company performance and well-being.

No single leader can meet the demands placed on them in isolation, and in order to succeed, they need to rely on a high-performance team to meet their goals. Unfortunately, most leadership literature and training focuses on helping leaders reach their potential. There is very little about leaders assisting teams to achieve their collective potential. Even though leadership is relational, requiring a leader, followers, and a shared objective, leadership does not reside in a figurehead. Everyone can and should lead.

Most people chronicle that they feel more engaged when working in a team that has clear objectives, works closely together to achieve those objectives, and meets regularly to review their performance and how they can improve it. Together, teams have more potential than individuals to overcome the challenges we face in business today. To do this, every team member should be involved in developing the vision and goals together. When collective leadership works, people are internally and externally motivated, working together towards a shared vision within a team.

Lasting success comes from the diverse perspectives and skills of many. Collective team leadership means leveraging all the members' unique talents and abilities to contribute to success. Collectively led teams think about the team first before the individuals. They realise that they are stronger together and recognise that sustainable change will be challenging to achieve without the strengths, perspectives, and efforts of many. To unleash the whole team's creativity, they need to tap into all the abilities and capabilities.

We often think of leaders as "hosts" rather than "heroes." Hosts use their skills to promote shared learning, effective team decision-making, reflection, visioning, goal setting, and mutual accountability. Hero leaders are expected to have all the answers all the time. Everyone brings them their problems to solve, and most of their time is spent fixing other people's mistakes.

In collectively-led teams, decision-making is shared or rotated. The leader is the process facilitator, but the team members make the recommendations for review and agreement by the whole team. Collective leadership recognises that people are inherently capable and can be trusted to do the right thing. In collectively led teams, there is shared responsibility for time management, focusing on goals, following up on results, decision-making, and resource management. They own the process in team meetings and the collective deliverables.

Shared learning and power, transparent and effective communication, and trust are essential to authentic engagement. Collective leadership recognises that people are inherently capable and can be trusted to do the right thing. The team should be a safe place to try and fail without criticism, to be creative, and to give and receive constructive feedback with respect.

As a mentor, I focus on helping teams effectively manage the expectations of all their stakeholders, run and transform the business simultaneously, manage their internal conflict positively, manage complexity, collaborate with other teams and individuals, stand back, reflect, and see the bigger picture, and build and sustain trust between colleagues.

Leadership and the Collective Mindset

Two leaders who have had a profound impact on their followers and societies are Anita Roddick, the founder of The Body Shop, and Rulon Timpson Jeffs, the leader of the Fundamentalist Church of Jesus Christ of Latter-Day Saints (FLDS).

Anita Roddick was a visionary leader whose commitment to ethical business practices and social responsibility transformed the beauty industry. She believed that business could be a force for good and that companies should be accountable for their impact on society and the environment. Roddick's leadership style was rooted in the empowerment of her employees and the communities her company served. She fostered a collective mindset that valued ethical consumption, environmental sustainability, and social justice. Her influence extended beyond The Body Shop, inspiring a generation of consumers and businesses to adopt more responsible practices. Roddick's leadership demonstrated how a positive collective mindset, driven by ethical values, can lead to widespread change and create a lasting legacy.

On the other hand, **Rulon Timpson Jeffs** led the FLDS with a very different approach. His leadership was characterised by authoritarian control and the enforcement of strict religious doctrines. Jeff's influence created a collective mindset among his followers that was insular, resistant to outside influence, and deeply rooted in fear and obedience. This mindset led to the perpetuation of practices that were harmful to the community, including polygamy and the suppression of individual freedoms. Jeff's leadership is a stark example of how a negative collective mindset can take root in a society and cause lasting damage.

These two leaders illustrate the profound impact that leadership can have on a group or society's collective mindset. While Roddick used her influence to foster a positive, ethical collective mindset, Jeff's leadership created an environment of control and fear, ultimately harming his followers.

Identifying Traits of Effective Leaders in Fostering a Positive Collective Mindset

In the leadership journey, the true essence of influence lies not in authority but in the ability to shape the hearts and minds of those we lead. The most effective leaders are those who cultivate a positive collective mindset within their organisations and communities—leaders who inspire, uplift, and transform. Such leaders possess certain defining traits that set them apart and create a ripple effect that extends far beyond their immediate sphere of influence.

Visionary Thinking:

A leader with visionary thinking sees beyond the present moment. They can cast a clear and compelling vision for the future, igniting their followers' imagination and passion. Visionary leaders understand that people are motivated by a sense of purpose and direction. They articulate their vision in a way that resonates with others, making it not just a possibility but a shared journey towards a common goal. By painting a vivid picture of what the future can be, they empower their teams to reach heights they never thought possible.

Empathy and Compassion:

Empathy is the bridge that connects a leader to their followers. An effective leader is deeply attuned to the needs, emotions, and aspirations of those they lead. They listen with the intent to understand, not just to respond. Compassionate leaders go beyond mere sympathy; they actively work to alleviate the challenges their people face. By prioritising the well-being of their team, they foster an environment of mutual respect and loyalty. In doing so, they build a foundation of trust that is essential for a positive collective mindset.

Ethical Integrity:

Integrity is the cornerstone of leadership. Leaders who operate with ethical integrity are guided by unwavering principles, even in the face of adversity. They do what is right, not what is easy or expedient. By leading with honesty and transparency, they create a culture of trust within their organisations. When leaders exemplify ethical behaviour, they set a standard for others to follow, reinforcing a collective mindset that values righteousness and accountability. Their integrity inspires confidence and ensures that the organisation remains steadfast in its moral commitments.

Empowerment:

Empowerment is a leader's gift to keep on giving. Effective leaders understand that their greatest legacy is not what they achieve themselves but what they enable others to achieve. They create opportunities for growth and development, equipping their followers with the skills, resources, and confidence they need to succeed. By encouraging innovation and creativity, they foster an environment where new ideas can flourish. Empowering leaders are not threatened by the success of others; rather, they celebrate it as a testament to their leadership. This approach not only drives individual success but also strengthens the collective mindset of the entire organisation.

Resilience and Adaptability:

Resilience is the hallmark of a leader who can weather the storms of change. In a world that is constantly evolving, the ability to adapt is crucial. Effective leaders are resilient in the face of challenges, viewing obstacles as opportunities for growth. They remain steadfast in their vision but are flexible in their approach. By demonstrating resilience and adaptability, they inspire their followers to do the same. They create a culture of perseverance, where setbacks are seen not as failures but as stepping-stones to greater success. This resilient mindset becomes embedded in the collective consciousness, enabling the organisation to thrive even in the most uncertain times.

Leadership Strategies for Building and Maintaining a Strong Group Culture

To cultivate a thriving group culture, leaders must not only embody these traits but also implement strategies that reinforce them within their organisations. Here are two essential strategies for building and maintaining a strong group culture:

Model the Desired Culture

Leadership is as much about action as it is about words. Leaders must be the living embodiment of the culture they wish to create. If a leader desires a culture of innovation, they must be willing to take risks and embrace new ideas. If they seek a culture of integrity, they must demonstrate ethical behaviour in every decision they make. By consistently modelling the desired culture, leaders set a powerful example for others to follow. This creates a domino effect, where the actions and values exhibited by the leader are mirrored by the entire organisation, solidifying a strong, cohesive culture.

Encourage Open Communication

Communication is the lifeblood of any organisation. Leaders who foster an environment of open dialogue create a culture of transparency and trust. Encouraging open communication means creating spaces where feedback is not only welcomed but valued. It means listening to concerns, ideas, and suggestions from all levels of the organisation. When leaders make it clear that every voice matters, they empower their followers to speak up, share their insights, and contribute to the collective good. This openness nurtures a culture of inclusivity and collaboration, where everyone feels heard, respected, and invested in the success of the group.

The Role of Governance in Shaping Ethical Leadership

Leadership, particularly in sectors that shape our values, ethics, and understanding of life, holds immense power over the collective mindset of society. Every government should recognise this influence and take active steps to ensure that those in positions of power uphold the highest standards of integrity and ethical responsibility. This is especially important for leaders in education, media, religious institutions, and public service—those who, whether directly or indirectly, mould the principles and behaviours of future generations. The potential risks of unchecked leadership influence, such as the spread of harmful ideologies or unethical practices, underscore the need for governance and accountability.

One crucial step is implementing policies or legislation that establish clear guidelines for leaders in these key sectors. These policies not only manage but actively guide leaders, ensuring that the messages they convey and the values they promote align with the well-being and long-term development of society. Just as a government's actions reflect a nation's character, its leaders' actions shape its citizens' moral fabric. The proactive role of policies in guiding leaders underlines the importance of governance in shaping ethical leadership.

Imagine a framework where every leader, particularly those who influence our values and ethics, is held accountable—not in a restrictive way that stifles creativity or freedom—but in a manner that ensures their influence contributes positively to the collective growth of society. Such governance would act as a safeguard, preventing the dissemination of harmful ideologies or unethical practices that could corrupt the minds of the people they are entrusted to guide.

This is not just about leadership in politics but in every sector that touches human development—education, media, religion, and business. Leaders in these fields shape more than policies; they shape minds. Their influence is profound, building or degrading a society's very essence. Therefore, they must be subject to oversight, with principles guiding what they should or should not promote.

A strong, value-driven society is built on ethical leadership. Leaders should be equipped with a deep understanding of their responsibility and constantly guided by policies that ensure their influence serves to elevate, rather than diminish, the people they lead. These leaders are the architects of our collective values and the stewards of our future, and as such, they must be carefully monitored, supported, and held accountable.

When we, as a society, demand that leadership is guided by integrity and responsibility, we can ensure that the values they propagate uplift individuals and, ultimately, the nation as a whole. Every individual we encounter, every success story or societal downfall, reflects the leadership that shaped them. Therefore, governments must take an active role in managing this leadership influence, not by controlling it but by ensuring that it remains a positive force for the collective good.

As we navigate the complexities of modern leadership, it is essential to remember that leadership is not just about decision-making—it is about influencing hearts and minds. When governments take proactive measures to manage and guide leaders, they safeguard the ethical foundation of society, ensuring that values are preserved and every leader's influence is channeled towards positive, meaningful change. True greatness in leadership lies not merely in wielding authority but in the wisdom to use that influence responsibly, always striving to uplift and empower the collective for the greater good.

Leadership influence has the power to create a collective mindset that shapes the society we live in. When leaders act with integrity and purpose, they inspire others to follow, fostering a culture of unity, trust, and shared values. As these values permeate communities, they form the foundation for a thriving, resilient society. The influence of leaders extends far beyond their immediate decisions—it moulds the collective's beliefs, attitudes, and actions, ultimately determining the direction of our future. The true impact of leadership lies not in personal gain, but in the lasting legacy it leaves in the hearts and minds of those it touches. This collective mindset strengthens and prepares society for a better tomorrow.

"Your attitude as a leader shapes the environment around you. Leadership doesn't just influence people; it transforms the whole environment." (S. Olamilekan Isreal)

CHAPTER 8

COMMUNICATION

The world's best leaders across all disciplines share a common trait: they are all exceptional communicators. Effective communication skills are the key to influencing and motivating groups of people, encouraging them to embrace an individual's beliefs, thoughts, ideas, theories, and even to achieve specific tasks.

On the other hand, many individuals who rely heavily on their knowledge and technical expertise in particular disciplines find themselves limited by poor communication skills. If these skills are not up to par, their abilities are undermined. Hence, being a skilled communicator is important in all aspects of life.

Whether in social or professional spheres, people spend a significant portion of their time interacting and dealing with others. Thus, being a skilled communicator becomes an essential component of success. This facilitates better comprehension of communication, leading to the achievement of objectives and progression towards goals.

Practical communication skills encompass various methods, including verbal expression and body language. These forms significantly influence how we communicate, underscoring the need to use these tools effectively to convey messages and receive feedback. Notably, the world's most eloquent speakers are clear and concise. As **Thomas Jefferson** wisely said, **"The most valuable of all talents is never using two words when one will do."**

Prominent communicators like Winston Churchill, Mahatma Gandhi, Prophet Muhammad, George Washington, Adolf Hitler, and Nelson Mandela stand out for their unique communication styles. These leaders all drove innovation and introduced new ideologies to the world. Despite the changing times, their communication methods remain unforgettable and invaluable.

Consider Mahatma Gandhi, born on October 2nd, 1869, in Porbandar, British India. Gandhi demonstrated effective communication in one of his notable speeches on January 4th,

1948, during a potential conflict between India and Pakistan. He began with a clear and concise introduction, addressing global concerns and then narrowing on the specific issue. By presenting a complete narrative and scenario, he effectively engaged his audience.

Gandhi delved into the details of actions taken by India and Pakistan while maintaining simplicity and clarity in his language. Despite his prestigious law degree from University College in London, he employed accessible language that resonated with his audience. This highlights the power of clear and concise communication.

The significance of body language in communication cannot be understated. Body language enhances message delivery and conveys content effectively. It guides the audience's focus to where the speaker intends. Adolf Hitler serves as an example of effective body language use.

Adolf Hitler, the German dictator who led the extremist Nazi party and served as Germany's chancellor-president from 1933 to 1945, was known for his passionate and impactful communication style. His mastery of body language and voice significantly influenced his rise to power. Hitler's oratory skills were honed by identifying clear speech objectives, understanding audience interests and motivations, and employing tools like posture, gesture, kinesics, body shape, appearance (such as his military attire), and voice modulation. His communication prowess garnered attention and influenced many.

Adolf Hitler's practical communication skills enabled him to become his party's most popular and impressive speaker. He exponentially increased the party's membership, inspiring followers who believed in his ideas and values. His success exemplifies how a skilled communicator can rally support and influence others.

In contrast, let us examine Mohamed Morsi, the fifth President of Egypt, who assumed office on June 30th, 2012. Morsi's communication skills faced challenges, as evidenced by his speech on December 5th, 2012, following the issuance of a constitutional manifesto that led to chaos and loss of lives.

Morsi's speech failed to address the critical objective of the constitutional manifesto. He glossed over relevant details, was unable to express regret for the lives lost, and neglected to acknowledge the gravity of the situation. Unlike Gandhi, who believed in the potential war's consequences, Morsi's communication lacked depth and resonance. His chief of staff's vague mention of "important news" without specification further weakened his speech's impact.

In contrast to Gandhi's empathetic tone and regret, Morsi's approach alienated many, causing increased opposition nationwide.

Effective communication requires understanding the audience's emotions, acknowledging their concerns, and using appropriate body language and voice modulation.

Communication is the lifeblood of any group, society, or organisation. The bridge connects individuals, enabling them to share ideas, express emotions, and work together towards common goals. However, the way we communicate is not just a matter of individual preference; it is deeply rooted in the collective mindset of the culture we belong to. This collective mindset, shaped by shared history, values, and experiences, significantly determines how we interact.

During my MBA program, an "Intercultural Communication" course profoundly impacted my understanding of how communication varies across cultural boundaries. This course taught me the importance of gaining competence in communicating effectively with people from diverse backgrounds. As the world becomes increasingly globalised, navigating these differences is crucial for building successful relationships, both in personal and professional settings.

Intercultural communication is vital because different cultures have distinct values, beliefs, and ways of reacting to situations. What might be considered polite or appropriate in one culture could be rude or unacceptable in another. This is where the idea of a collective mindset becomes essential. A collective mindset is a shared way of thinking and behaving passed down through generations within a culture. It influences everything from how we communicate to how we perceive the world.

The Russian Style of Communication

Let us consider the case of Russia to understand how a collective mindset shapes communication. Russians are known for their direct and often blunt communication style. This can be traced back to their collective mindset, shaped by centuries of history, including periods of hardship, war, and strong central authority. The Russian mindset values strength, resilience, and clarity. As a result, their communication tends to be straightforward, with little room for ambiguity.

In Russian culture, there is a saying, **"Words are silver, silence is gold."** This reflects a deep respect for the power of words and a preference for meaningful, well-considered speech over unnecessary chatter. Russians often communicate in a manner that may seem brusque to outsiders, but within their cultural context, it is a sign of respect and seriousness. This directness is rooted in their collective experience and has become a defining feature of their communication style.

Understanding the Russian approach to communication highlights the importance of recognising and respecting the collective mindsets of different cultures. It also underscores the need for adaptability in communication, especially when engaging with people from diverse backgrounds.

The Role of Effective Communication in Shaping Collective Mindsets

Effective communication is not just about exchanging information; it is about building connections and fostering understanding. In any group or society, how people communicate can strengthen the collective mindset or create barriers that hinder progress. When communication is open, honest, and respectful, it helps to reinforce shared values and goals. This, in turn, strengthens the collective mindset and creates a sense of unity and purpose.

However, communication can also be a double-edged sword. Misunderstandings, misinterpretations, and cultural differences can create barriers that lead to conflict and division. It is essential to develop cultural awareness and sensitivity to overcome these barriers. By understanding the collective mindsets of different cultures, we can tailor our communication to be more effective and inclusive.

Overcoming Barriers to Communication

One of the most significant barriers to effective communication is the assumption that everyone thinks and communicates the same way we do. This is rarely the case. It is important to approach communication with an open mind and a willingness to learn from others to overcome this barrier.

Here are some practical techniques for improving group communication:

1. **Active Listening**: Truly listen to what others say without interrupting or making assumptions. This shows respect and helps to build trust.

2. **Cultural Awareness**: Learn about the cultural backgrounds of the people you are communicating with. This will help you understand their communication style and avoid misunderstandings.

3. **Clarity and Simplicity**: It is important to be clear and concise when communicating across cultural boundaries. Avoid using jargon or idiomatic expressions that everyone may not understand.

4. **Feedback and Reflection**: Encourage open feedback to ensure your message is understood as intended. Reflect on your communication style and be willing to make adjustments as needed.

5. **Patience and Flexibility:** Communication across cultures can be challenging, but patience and flexibility can help overcome obstacles. Be prepared to adapt your communication style to better suit the needs of your audience.

Building a Strong Communication Culture

If we want to influence the way we communicate, we must be willing to change our behaviour. As our children grow older, they naturally adopt the communication styles they observe. Our cultural differences influence our current communication patterns. To communicate more effectively, we need to adjust our mindset to match the desired outcome.

In any group or society, fostering a culture of effective communication is critical to sustaining a positive collective mindset. Leaders play a crucial role in this process by modelling the desired communication conducts and encouraging others to do the same. By creating an environment where open dialogue is valued and differences are respected, leaders can help to build a strong, cohesive culture that supports the growth and development of all its members.

Communication is more than just the exchange of words; it is a powerful tool that shapes our collective mindset and influences the way we interact with the world. By understanding the impact of culture on communication and taking steps to improve our communication skills, we can create more meaningful connections, foster greater understanding, and build stronger, more resilient communities.

> *"The way we communicate is not just a matter of individual preference; it is deeply rooted in the collective mindset of the culture we belong to." (S. Olamilekan Isreal)*

CHAPTER 9

GROWTH AND DEVELOPMENT

Have you ever wondered why growth and development are perceived as threats in certain societies or why some individuals resist personal evolution? Or perhaps you have questioned why some organisations stagnate, failing to adapt or improve over time. The answer lies in a powerful yet often invisible force: "The collective mindset." This shared mentality, deeply ingrained in a group or society, can either propel or stifle progress.

Throughout my journey, I have encountered societies that resist change, individuals who reject personal growth, and organisations that are impervious to innovation. What do they all have in common? A collective mindset that clings to the familiar and resists the unknown. This mindset can be so entrenched that those within it see any attempt at growth as a threat to their identity, values, or way of life.

Take the story of Compaq, once a leading computer manufacturer. Compaq was a trailblazer in the early days of the personal computer revolution, but as the industry evolved, the company struggled to adapt. Despite its early success, Compaq failed to embrace the rapid technological advancements and shifts in consumer preferences. The company's leadership was hesitant to change its business model, preferring to adhere to what had worked in the past. This resistance to growth and development led to Compaq's decline and eventual acquisition by Hewlett-Packard, a company that had successfully navigated the industry's changes.

Similarly, General Motors (GM), one of the giants of the automotive industry, found itself in a precarious position for similar reasons. For decades, GM was the epitome of American industrial might. However, as the global market shifted and new competitors emerged, GM's reluctance to innovate and adapt to changing consumer demands and environmental regulations led to significant losses. The company's failure to embrace growth and development, both in terms of technology and organisational culture, ultimately led to its bankruptcy and the need for a government bailout.

On a national level, we can look at Benin, a country rich in history and culture, but one that has struggled with growth and development. Despite its potential, Benin's economy has been hampered by a collective mindset that resists modernisation and change. The country's leadership and populace have often prioritised maintaining traditional ways of life over embracing new opportunities for economic and social advancement. This resistance has kept Benin from realising its full potential, leaving it lagging behind other nations that have been more open to growth and development.

The consequences of rejecting growth and development are clear. Societies, people, and organisations that resist change ultimately find themselves left behind, unable to compete or thrive in a rapidly evolving world. This resistance stems from a fear of the unknown, a desire to maintain the status quo or a lack of vision. But without growth, there can be no progress, and without progress, stagnation sets in.

Embracing a growth mindset is the antidote to this stagnation. A growth mindset fosters curiosity, innovation, and resilience. It allows individuals and groups to see challenges as opportunities rather than threats and to view failure as a stepping-stone to success. This mindset is not just about personal development; it is essential for the growth of organisations and societies as well.

A collective mindset that embraces growth and development can transform a group or society. It encourages continuous improvement, lifelong learning, and a willingness to adapt to new circumstances. This mindset is evident in many of the world's most successful organisations and communities. For example, companies like Google and Apple have thrived by fostering cultures of innovation and continuous learning. They encourage their employees to take risks, learn from failure, and constantly seek new improvement methods.

To cultivate a growth-oriented collective mindset, it is essential to implement strategies prioritising continuous improvement and lifelong learning, such as fostering curiosity, promoting ongoing education, and embracing change as a catalyst for growth. Leaders must also lead by example, demonstrating a commitment to development and collaboration, thereby inspiring others to pursue knowledge and innovation.

Leaders who adopt a growth mindset will multiply their team's potential and create a healthy culture of accountability that drives business growth.

A leader with a growth mindset sees opportunities for their team, even during times of crisis. They do not curl up in a corner believing all efforts have been wasted and do not look for anyone to blame. Instead, they try to accelerate their team's growth to overcome any business challenge.

Let us examine Scaling Up Sherpa Kids in Ireland:

Dawn Engelbrecht, Managing Director of Sherpa Kids International, has been the driving force behind the sKids and Sherpa Kids businesses growing from ten sites in New Zealand to over 260 worldwide in just 20 years.

What was her secret? She had a growth mindset, which she also led her team to adopt. Take a look at how she helped just one of her team members, John Miles, expand Sherpa Kids throughout Ireland.

When John became Ireland's master franchisor of Sherpa Kids, he had over 20 years of experience working as a financier on Wall Street in London but no experience in childcare. He was also in his 50s—an age when most people would be planning their retirement, not starting a new business.

Someone with a fixed mindset would probably think that John does not have what it takes to succeed in the childcare franchise business. After all, his talents and professional experience are in finance, and he should be retiring, right?

Thankfully, Dawn believed in John's passion and capability for growth. She guided and encouraged John to develop new skills to scale Sherpa Kids in Ireland.

Even John himself was sceptical that he could learn new skills. But thanks to Dawn's belief in him, he decided to join the course she recommended. "I'll give it a go. Maybe you can teach an old dog new tricks," John recalls his decision.

Developing new skills was everything for John. He said, "It gave me better clarity. It's not just knowing that I want to go from A to B. Now, I know how we'll get there, what road we'll be taking, and most importantly, what vehicle we're taking and who's in the car with me. I also have more time in my business and life."

How did John's growth impact Sherpa Kids?

Well, John went on to help Sherpa Kids rise in Ireland. He gained new inquiries from potential franchisees of Sherpa Kids, from Derry to Cork and Dublin to Galway. With a real demand for this product or service offering and with newfound clarity, John set out to work towards expanding Sherpa Kids into all 32 counties of Ireland within five years.

This achievement was only made possible thanks to Dawn's growth mindset, which supported and inspired her team to develop their talent and scale the business.

Dawn and John's story shows how leaders who push forward with a growth mindset inspire their teams to do the same.

Leading with a growth mindset is critical to developing your team into proactive, accountable, and motivated solution-seekers. As your team grows and evolves, so will the company.

Soon enough, you will have created a culture of people who are open to feedback, accountable for their own evolution, and resilient enough to take on new challenges, all of which promote innovation and business growth.

However, refusing to embrace growth and development can have dire consequences for individuals, organisations, and societies. The stories of Compaq, General Motors, and Benin illustrate the dangers of clinging to the past and resisting change. However, we can unlock our full potential and achieve lasting success by cultivating a collective mindset that values growth, continuous improvement, and lifelong learning.

> *"A Growth mindset allows individuals and groups to see challenges as opportunities rather than threats and to view failure as a stepping-stone to success."*

TRUST AND COLLABORATION

Trust and collaboration are the twin pillars that uphold any successful collective endeavour. Without trust, collaboration is hollow; without collaboration, trust is aimless. The synergy between these two forces is vital for achieving any shared vision or goal. But why do so many groups, organisations, and societies struggle to harness this powerful dynamic? The answer lies in the power of a collective mindset.

A collective mindset is the shared attitude, beliefs, and values that shape how a group thinks, communicates, and, ultimately, collaborates. The unseen force drives the level of trust within a group and determines how effectively members can work together. When a group shares a positive and forward-thinking collective mindset, trust becomes the natural foundation upon which collaboration is built. However, when the collective mindset is fragmented or misaligned, trust erodes, and collaboration falters.

Over a century ago, Abraham Lincoln was assassinated, and it so happens that Lincoln and his Secretary of War, the short and sturdy Edwin Stanton, set the highest standard of collaboration I know.

Four things stand out in the way the two men worked together to lead the US through the civil war:

1. Lincoln and Stanton reached results because they turned their differences into strengths

To strengthen this position, read how Stanton's private secretary, A.E., described the team in 1891:

"No two men were ever more utterly and irreconcilably unlike. The secretiveness Lincoln wholly lacked, Stanton had in marked degree; the charity, which Stanton could not feel, coursed from every pore in Lincoln. Lincoln was for giving a wayward subordinate seventy times seven chances to repair his errors; Stanton was for either forcing him to obey or cutting off his head without more ado. Lincoln was as calm and unruffled as the summer sea in moments of the greatest peril; Stanton would lash himself into a fury over the same condition of things. Stanton would take hardships with a groan; Lincoln would find a funny story to fit them. Stanton was all dignity and sternness, Lincoln all simplicity and good nature… yet no two men ever did or could work better in harness. They supplemented each other's nature, and they fully recognised the fact that they were a necessity to each other."

2. Lincoln always backed Stanton up in public, even if most of his decisions were unpopular (and that is an understatement)

"I cannot add to Mr. Stanton's troubles. His position is one of the most difficult in the world. Thousands in the army blame him because they are not promoted and other thousands out of the army blame him because they are not appointed. The pressure upon him is immeasurable and unending. He is the rock on the beach of our national ocean against which the breakers dash and roar without ceasing. He fights back the angry waters and prevents them from undermining and overwhelming the land. Gentlemen, I do not see how he survives or why he is not crushed and torn. Without him, I would be destroyed. He performs his task superhumanly. Do not mind this matter, for Mr. Stanton is right, and I cannot wrongly interfere with him."

3. Lincoln used the power of humour to get his way when needed

Or how is this for an effective order: "Appoint this man, regardless of whether he knows the colour of Julius Caesar's hair or not." A. Lincoln.

4. The Lincoln-Stanton collaboration was based on mutual trust

Here is the letter Stanton, devastated by Lincoln's death, received from Lincoln's private secretary, John Hay:

> "Not everyone knows, as I do, how close you stood to our lost leader, how he loved you and trusted you, and how in vain were all the efforts to shake that trust and confidence, not lightly given and never withdrawn. All this will be known sometime, to his honour and yours."

How did the two men, you might wonder, get to know each other?

They first met during the trial of a patent case six years before Lincoln was elected president. Lincoln, then an unknown lawyer, had worked day and night in preparation of his speech for the defendant. When he wanted to introduce himself to

Stanton (the lead counsel), he was greeted with the words, "Why is this long-armed ape here?" Stanton was educated at a fine university (Lincoln was self-taught) and did not hide that he looked down on Lincoln. He refused to let him give his speech. He never asked him out for lunch. He ignored him the entire trial.

Why did Lincoln, hurt and humiliated to the bone, sit down on his pride when he needed a Secretary of War? Why did he call Stanton to the White House six years later? Because he had seen how persistent and talented he was, he knew he would be the right man for the job. Now, that is collaborative leadership. That is why Lincoln still serves as an excellent example for executive leaders among us today.

"Now he belongs to the ages," Stanton said when Lincoln passed away in the Petersen boarding house across Ford's Theatre on April 15, 1865. So, think about Lincoln and how he mastered the art of collaboration, and let this story inspire you and many generations to come.

Take Google, for example—a company that has mastered the art of fostering trust and collaboration within its ranks. Google's success is not just a result of brilliant ideas or cutting-edge technology; it is deeply rooted in a collective mindset that values openness, innovation, and mutual respect. By creating an environment where employees feel trusted and empowered, Google has built a culture of collaboration that drives continuous improvement and success. Their collective mindset encourages sharing, openness to ideas, and a belief in the team's collective power, not just the individual.

However, not all collaborations are successful, as the case of Kraft and Starbucks illustrates. When these two giants partnered in 1998, the goal was to bring Starbucks coffee into grocery stores across America. Initially, the collaboration seemed like a perfect match—Kraft had the distribution power, and Starbucks had the brand appeal. However, as time went on, the partnership began to deteriorate. The issue was not just about operational disagreements; it was rooted in a fundamental misalignment in their collective mindset.

Kraft viewed the partnership as a long-term, stable venture, whereas Starbucks was more aggressive, focused on rapid growth and maintaining control over its brand. As Starbucks started to grow, it felt constrained by Kraft's traditional and slower approach, leading to friction between the two companies. Trust began to erode as each party's differing goals and values came to the forefront. Eventually, this lack of confidence and alignment in their collective mindset led to the dissolution of the partnership in 2010, with Starbucks paying Kraft nearly three billion dollars in damages for breach of contract. This collaboration once held so much promise and ended in a bitter and costly legal battle.

This story of Kraft and Starbucks underscores the importance of trust and a shared collective mindset in any collaboration. No matter how strong a partnership may appear on the surface if the underlying values and goals are not aligned, the partnership is likely to fail. Trust cannot be mandated or manufactured; it must be cultivated. It grows when individuals believe in the vision and purpose of the group and when they see their leaders and peers embodying the principles that go in line with that vision. Trust is strengthened when there is transparency in communication, consistency in action, and fairness in decision-making. It is through this trust that collaboration thrives, leading to successful outcomes.

However, the lack of a strong collective mindset can have devastating effects. In some societies and organisations, the absence of trust stifles collaboration before it even begins. I have seen this firsthand in my own country, where long-term visions are often dismissed because they do not immediately correspond with the prevailing mindset that prioritises short-term gains. Here, the collective mindset is skewed towards immediate financial reward, leaving little room for collaboration on projects that require patience and sustained effort. This mindset not only hinders trust but also prevents individuals and groups from working together towards the greater good.

For example, when I embarked on a new business venture with a vision focused on ethical practices and long-term impact, I was met with scepticism. Despite assembling a team and clearly articulating our goals, the collective mindset—deeply rooted in quick wins and immediate gratification—caused friction. Trust was lacking because the vision did not coordinate with the prevailing mindset. As a result, collaboration was ineffective, and the initiative faltered.

This experience taught me that for any vision to be realised, it must be supported by a collective mindset that fosters trust. Collaboration cannot thrive in an environment where trust is absent, and trust cannot exist without a shared belief in the vision. Therefore, if we are to pursue our goals with any hope of success, we must seek out and work with individuals who share a mindset that moves with our vision. Only then can we build the trust necessary to collaborate effectively.

The collective mindset is the driving force behind trust and collaboration in any group, society, or organisation. It shapes how individuals perceive each other, how they communicate, and how they work together to achieve common goals. Without a strong collective mindset, trust is fragile, and collaboration is ineffective.

The stories of Google, Kraft, and Starbucks illustrate the profound impact that the collective mindset can have on the success or failure of collaboration. While Google's alignment and culture of trust have propelled it to the forefront of innovation, the misalignment between Kraft and Starbucks led to a costly and failed partnership. These examples serve as powerful reminders that trust and collaboration are not just about good intentions—they are about cultivating a shared mindset that aligns with the vision and values of the group.

As we move forward in our personal and professional lives, let us remember the importance of nurturing a collective mindset that fosters trust, embraces collaboration, and respects the diverse contributions of every individual. By doing so, we can create environments where collaboration thrives, trust is unwavering, and extraordinary achievements are not just possible but inevitable.

> *"When a group shares a positive and forward-thinking collective mindset, trust becomes the natural foundation upon which collaboration is built."*
> *(S. Olamilekan Isreal)*

CHAPTER 11

INFLUENCE

Influence is a double-edged sword that cuts deep into the fabric of our lives, often in ways that we barely perceive. Its impact is subtle yet profound, an invisible force that shapes our thoughts, actions, and, ultimately, our destiny. Influence, much like leadership, is a force to be reckoned with. Just as leadership can mould our mindset and environment, influence echoes that leadership—the lasting impression it leaves on us all.

Leadership and influence are inseparable, like Siamese twins. A leader's accurate measure lies in the influence they wield—whether they are celebrated or criticised depends on the nature of that influence. Leadership is the fire that ignites change, while influence is the smoke that spreads through the air, permeating our environment. Like smoke, influence can pollute or purify, leading us to greatness or dragging us down into chaos.

For decades, influence has been the driving force behind our collective mindset. It shapes how we think, act, and perceive the world. What we see, hear, and experience can uplift or hold us back. The essence of influence is rooted in our mindset; it is our mindset that gives rise to influence, shaping our culture and lives. Without a strong foundation of positive thinking, influence can become a destructive force, replicating harmful patterns and reinforcing negative behaviours.

Becoming influential is one part talent and the other part timing. It has to do with taking opportunities at the right time. When influence is given, it is a blessing from God and a great responsibility. Therefore, anyone deemed influential must cherish it and use it to transform society and the world into a better, kinder, and more human place.

"We must be the change we want to see."
(Mahatma Gandhi)

Being named as an influential person is not merely an accolade but a call to action.

Recently, I saw a report that a Syrian boy picked up one euro on the road and decided to donate it to the Taiwanese to buy vaccines. Living as a Syrian refugee is undoubtedly a difficult situation, but he was willing to donate this one euro, which shows that he has chosen a different path in life. It demonstrates that he decides to shoulder even more responsibilities than the average person by paying it forward.

No one is born as a leader. No one can make you a leader. No title can mark you as a leader. All of us can play the passive role of a victim or lead by example. Gandhi is a perfect example of the latter. Gandhi's stature and influence were so widespread, as seen by the adoption of his principles by political activists such as Martin Luther King Jr.

"Christ gave us the goals and Mahatma Gandhi the tactics." (Martin Luther King Jr)

Recognising the need of the hour and seizing the opportunity head-on with all sincerity is what made Gandhi a great and beloved leader. Focus was another great virtue through which he garnered much attention as an informal authoritarian. Freedom was the epicentre of his attention. This was on the same lines as Margret Sanger on birth control as a woman's choice in the US. Gandhi believed and lived by bringing about change through Satyagraha: non-violent civil disobedience. He brought about the independence of India (the world's largest economy at that time) by influencing millions of people who resonated with this inner conviction on non-violent tactics.

He was a great statesman and a man of vision. He associated himself with Indians as slaves to British rule, which automatically made him one among the millions of people yearning for freedom and oppressed by the barbaric rule of the British. He was a transformational leader who gave hope to followers when there was none, thus inspiring them towards success.

The Different Types of Influence

Influence manifests in various forms, each playing a critical role in shaping our collective mindset and the dynamics of our groups. The key types of influence include:

1. Leadership Influence:

Leadership influence is perhaps the most potent influence. It involves the ability of leaders to inspire, motivate, and guide others towards a common goal. A leader's vision, decisions, and behaviours set the tone for the entire group, shaping its culture and direction. Leaders like Martin Luther King Jr demonstrated how leadership influence can uplift and unify, fostering a collective mindset of justice and equality. Conversely, leaders like Adolf Hitler exemplify how leadership influence can be wielded destructively, leading to devastating consequences.

On a personal level, I am a testament to the profound impact of leadership influence. I always felt a deep love for God from a young age, though it was more out of recognition than understanding. Before my encounter with the Holy Spirit, my life was chaotic, shaped by the various negative influences around me. Everything changed once I realised that the mindset I had adopted was leading me towards the destruction of my purpose. I experienced a newfound peace and an intense desire to serve God more fervently.

However, I also recognised that I was unprepared—a raw material needing refinement. Aware of this, God began orchestrating a plan to guide my transformation. One afternoon, during a brief nap, the Holy Spirit directed me to attend a Bible school and find a place of worship. Initially, I was anxious and unsure of where to start, but my wife reassured me that everything would fall into place when the time was right. We decided to search for a church the following Sunday. I unexpectedly ran into an old friend at a grocery store that same day. We had lost contact for years, but he was now deeply involved with a local church. He invited me to attend their upcoming retreat, and I enthusiastically agreed, not yet realising this was the Holy Spirit's work.

My family and I felt an overwhelming sense of belonging at the retreat. During the service, the pastor announced that the Bible school form was available for the new session. It was then that I realised the Holy Spirit had been guiding me all along. Without hesitation, I enrolled in the school and became a full member of Winners Chapel Ministry. My journey through Bible school was transformative. The teachings of Bishop David Oyedepo became my anchor, and I immersed myself in his sermons and writings. His mentorship, though distant, opened my eyes to the deeper truths of Christianity and leadership. I started spending more time in fellowship with the Holy Spirit, reading books, and growing in knowledge, knowing I was destined to lead. Throughout my time at the Bible school, the Holy Spirit was my constant guide, making learning more accessible and more profound.

I graduated as the best student in my class, a testament to the Holy Spirit's role as the ultimate teacher (John 14:26). This journey opened my eyes to see life differently. Though it was not easy—I faced moments of deep regret, weakness, and tears—I continually reminded myself of God's love and the purpose behind my past experiences. He reassured me that my past mistakes were part of a more excellent plan, preparing me for the tasks ahead. My past mistakes were primarily a result of negative influence, but I was able to rescue myself through the power of switching my mindset. When rooted in the correct principles, leadership influence can transform lives, just as it transformed mine.

2. Peer Influence:

Peer influence operates within groups, where individuals influence each other's behaviours, attitudes, and beliefs. This form of influence can be potent because it is often subtle and pervasive. In a positive environment, peer influence can encourage collaboration, innovation, and mutual support. However, in a negative context, it can lead to conformity, groupthink, and the perpetuation of harmful practices. The culture within a team or organisation often directly reflects the prevailing peer influence.

The challenge with individuals who remain resistant to change, despite your best efforts to help them understand the consequences of their behaviour, often stems from the collective mindset they are part of. The solution lies in actively disengaging from these limiting perspectives. By consciously avoiding what you do not wish to see, hear, or be associated with and maintaining this stance over time, you can gradually cultivate a new culture and mindset. Eventually, what once seemed distant or irrelevant becomes part of your reality, allowing you to engage with it without being influenced. This process of exclusion and adoption leads to a transformative shift, enabling you to master and redefine your environment through a renewed mindset.

3. Cultural Influence:

Cultural influence encompasses the values, norms, and practices shared by a community or society. It shapes how individuals perceive the world and their place in it. Cultural influence can be a force for good, promoting unity and shared identity, but it can also perpetuate stereotypes, biases, and resistance to change. A society's collective mindset is primarily shaped by its cultural influence, which affects everything from public policy to social interactions.

4. Organisational Influence:

Within organisations, influence is exerted through formal and informal channels. Formal influence comes from policies, procedures, and leadership directives, while informal influence arises from the company's culture, traditions, and unwritten rules. Organisational influence determines how employees interact, make decisions, and contribute to the company's goals. A positive organisational influence encourages creativity, accountability, and ethical behaviour, whereas a toxic influence can lead to dysfunction, low morale, and high turnover.

Influence in Action: Lessons from History

A striking example of negative influence can be found in the history of Adolf Hitler. Hitler's toxic ideology and charismatic leadership led to one of the darkest chapters in human history. His influence was so pervasive that it resulted in the devastation of entire nations and the loss of millions of lives. Hitler's legacy serves as a grim reminder of how influence, when rooted in a flawed and destructive mindset, can lead to catastrophic consequences for individuals and societies alike.

In contrast, the life and work of Martin Luther King Jr. exemplify the power of positive influence. King's vision of equality, justice, and non-violence inspired a movement that transformed the United States and inspired people worldwide. His influence was a force for good, rooted in a mindset of compassion, integrity, and hope. King's legacy is a testament to the fact that when harnessed for the right purposes, influence can uplift entire communities and create lasting change.

These examples illustrate the profound impact of influence on our collective mindset. Whether in a negative or positive light, influence shapes the dynamics of groups, organisations, and societies. It is a potent force that can drive success or precipitate failure, depending on how it is wielded.

The Role of Influence in Collaboration: The Kraft and Starbucks Example:

Influence also plays a crucial role in the success or failure of collaborations. A poignant example of this is the failed partnership between Kraft and Starbucks. Initially, this collaboration seemed promising, with Kraft responsible for distributing Starbucks coffee in grocery stores. However, as time passed, differing visions and priorities between the two companies led to friction. Kraft's traditional, conservative approach clashed with Starbucks' dynamic and rapidly evolving brand strategy. This misalignment, fueled by a breakdown in trust and communication, ultimately led to the partnership's demise. What began as a potentially lucrative collaboration ended in a costly legal battle and a severed relationship.

This example underscores the importance of aligning influence with shared goals and values in any collaborative effort. Even the most promising collaborations can falter without a strong, positive influence guiding the partnership.

Harnessing Positive Influence for Success

To harness the power of influence for positive outcomes, it is crucial to be mindful of the influences we allow into our lives and our impact on others. This involves cultivating a mindset prioritising growth, collaboration, and ethical leadership. Leaders must recognise the responsibility of their role and strive to be sources of positive influence.

Strategies for harnessing positive influence include fostering open communication, promoting shared goals, and leading by example. Creating environments where peer influence supports collective success rather than undermining it is also essential. In organisations, for instance, encouraging collaboration and mutual respect can lead to innovative solutions and more robust team dynamics.

However, when influence is misaligned with the group or society's values, the results can be disastrous. A poignant example of this is the failed collaboration between Kraft and Starbucks. What began as a promising partnership ended in a legal battle and a severed relationship, mainly due to misaligned goals and a breakdown of trust. This serves as a cautionary tale of how influence, when not carefully managed, can lead to counterproductive and damaging outcomes.

Influence is the lifeblood of leadership and the cornerstone of our collective mindset. Whether it leads to growth or decline depends on the attitude from which it stems. As leaders and individuals, we must be vigilant about the influences we embrace and our impact on those around us. By fostering a positive and growth-oriented mindset, we can ensure that our influence leads to a brighter future for all.

"Mindset gives birth to influence, and influence shapes culture. Mindset forms the foundation of every culture, and the culture created by your mindset determines the outcomes you experience today."
(S. Olamilekan Isreal)

CHAPTER 12

FAMILY

I vividly remember the day I first enrolled in high school. My mother accompanied me to take the entrance examination, and when we arrived, I was struck by the sight of hundreds of other kids also there to take the test. After we finished the exam, I observed the behaviour of some of the other kids. Some were acting rough, others were well-composed, and some fell in between—what I called the "Men in the Middle." They were not overly rough, nor were they mainly composed.

This made me wonder why different kids behave and act so differently in school. I guess we have all asked about it at some point. One possible reason is the influence of the parental pattern—the collective mindset that has shaped these kids into who they are.

One of the most challenging moments for me was officially starting high school. It was not easy at first to relate to some of the kids because their attitudes and ways of thinking differed significantly from mine. I remember getting into a fight with one of the more challenging kids. These tough kids usually sat at the back of the class, and they would try to copy you during exams. If you resisted, they would bully you or even beat you up.

Though this experience was challenging and not particularly favourable, it taught me one of the greatest lessons of my life: how to connect and interact with people with different attitudes and mindsets. It was an unforgettable situation that helped shape my understanding of human behaviour and the profound impact that a collective mindset, often rooted in parental influence, can have on a child's development.

Some children hesitate to pursue their dreams because of a collective mindset ingrained by family. Many give up on themselves, unaware of their vast potential and how far they could go if only they could break free from the limiting beliefs inherited from their family.

Not long ago, I found a biscuit wrapper tucked away in my child's jacket—a small yet profound reminder of their commitment to responsible behaviour. Each time they embrace this tradition, I am reminded of the importance of passing down values from generation to generation.

A nation reflects the collective values upheld by the families within it. Consider Japan: its greatness stems from the robust and functional family units contributing to an organised society. In contrast, many African nations struggle because they have more families with weakened value systems. It is a simple equation: positive change begins with just one child whose parents decide to teach them differently, igniting a chain reaction of social transformation.

Children often mirror their parents' sins and lifestyles. Forces at work can lead them down the same paths, which underscores the spiritual responsibility parents have for their children. If parents open the door to negativity in their lives, that negativity can seep into their children's lives. We must remember that our role as parents is to guide and nurture, providing a foundation that fosters strength and resilience.

Papa Jesse exemplifies outstanding parenting, having shaped his sons with love and wisdom. David, the anointed king, enjoyed the unwavering support of his brothers—evidence of a family raised in harmony.

A country is essentially a mosaic of families, each with its own values and beliefs. Thus, the strength of a nation is directly linked to the integrity of its families. If we desire to build a better nation, we must start at the family level, nurturing strong values such as honesty, respect, fairness, and accountability. These principles are essential in creating a society rich in spiritual depth and national pride.

No nation can realise its potential without a shared ethos cultivated through family teachings over time. The family is the first agent of socialisation, instilling foundational ideals before individuals enter the broader world of schools and communities.

To truly transform our societies, we must prioritise the development of families that embody these core values. A strong family not only cultivates good citizens but also fosters a spirit of patriotism and cooperation, shaping a brighter future for all.

Culturally, parenting practices vary widely. In many African societies, for example, a collectivist approach emphasises communal responsibility in raising children. This often includes teaching children resilience through adversity—preparing them for a better tomorrow.

Experts agree that a nurturing family environment is crucial for a child's development. Parents are the first educators, setting the stage for moral behaviour and character. A fractured family can lead to societal issues, producing individuals who may become societal burdens rather than contributors.

The family is the cornerstone of personal growth and fulfilment. When families falter, society pays the price. Education and guidance have increasingly shifted away from the home, leading to a reliance on institutions that can never replace the family's unique role.

The family is a divine institution, the bedrock upon which society is built. When families thrive, so does society; when they struggle, society suffers. Efforts to address societal issues without addressing family dynamics are short-sighted. Historically, the importance of family was recognised long before social sciences began to study it in depth.

In the Bible, we see the family established as fundamental to our existence. Jesus entered the world through a family, underscoring its significance in His teachings. He often spoke of family in his parables, such as the story of the Prodigal Son, which illustrates the enduring bond of love and forgiveness within a family.

A well-balanced family environment fosters growth. It requires the right blend of dependence and independence, freedom, and responsibility. Building a strong family takes dedication, love, and hard work—but the rewards are immeasurable. In a supportive family, members learn to navigate life's challenges together, providing warmth and encouragement.

Strong families communicate openly, ensuring every voice is heard and respected. Improving listening skills among family members is crucial to fostering deep connections and relationships. Affection and attention are essential; after all, strong relationships, including those within families, need nurturing.

Moreover, families serve as centres of creativity where individual gifts can flourish. A child's family is the most significant influence on their life, shaping character and values. In the home, we learn that people matter more than possessions—a lesson best imparted through daily interactions.

As the Bible advises, **"Train up a child in the way he should go; even when he is old, he will not depart from it"** **Proverbs 22:6.** While peers and institutions play important roles in a child's life, the home remains the heart of character development. Moral values and character are often "caught" rather than "taught."

No family is perfect, and every family faces its share of challenges. Marriage unites two imperfect people, but with commitment and love, families can weather the storms of life. Strong families support one another through difficulties, maintaining their bonds even in tough times. Instead of letting challenges tear them apart, they come together, finding solutions and growing more potent as a unit.

However, the path to a prosperous society lies in our families. Investing in substantial, value-driven families builds a brighter future for everyone. Let us recognise the power of family as the foundation of our nation and commit to nurturing and supporting one another for generations to come.

Inherited Mindset: The Foundation of a Collective Mindset

A collective mindset cannot emerge without an inherited mindset at its core. A family's mindset is passed down through generations, forming the collective mindset that shapes society today. The inherited mindset is the cause and the curse of many societal patterns we observe. The ancestral foundation gives birth to the collective mindset, much like how specific genetic traits are passed down from parents to children.

An inherited mindset is deeply ingrained and difficult to break free from. A collective mindset does not just exist independently; these inherited beliefs and values sustain it. That is why it is called an inherited mindset.

What everyone learns from their generational background becomes part of their collective mindset. This inherited mindset is so influential that it affects even those outside its original generational context. As people adopt these mindsets, they pass them down to their children, who then pass them down to their own. This cycle shapes the society we live in today.

Changing the minds of many parents is challenging because they see their inherited mindset as an unbreakable link to their family roots. They pass these beliefs down to their children, and the chain continues.

Inherited mindsets shape our traditions; one essential resource for breaking free from them is self-discipline. Self-discipline is crucial for being different and better than before. Changing an inherited mindset is hard work; it requires strict self-discipline and dedication. As individuals adopt new ways of thinking, their perspectives shift, affecting the collective mindset.

The more the inherited mindset evolves, the more the collective mindset will change. For example, many women might appreciate the wrong men over the right ones due to the inherited mindset that has shaped their perspective on love and relationships. A child born into such a family will only know and express love based on the mindset she has inherited from her parents and the teachings she constantly receives.

Some children hesitate to pursue their dreams because

of a collective mindset ingrained by family. Many give up on themselves, unaware of their vast potential and how far they could go if only they could break free from the limiting beliefs inherited from their family.

A few years ago, I met an extraordinary young woman named Rebecca. In her late 20s, Rebecca had already graduated from a prestigious university full of intellect and ambition. She appeared to have it all together on the surface, but beneath her accomplishments, she carried a burdened heart.

During one of our conversations, Rebecca opened up about her painful past. As a child, she had been wrongly exposed sexually, and with no one to confide in, she kept much of her pain bottled up. Although her parents were physically present, they overlooked the most crucial aspects of her emotional well-being. Lacking the proper guidance she desperately needed, Rebecca became vulnerable to her environment, eventually leading her down a path of destruction.

She shared with me how, at a very young age, she was introduced to smoking and drinking. Before long, these habits escalated to more dangerous activities, such as drug abuse. Rebecca's life became a whirlwind of reckless behavior, although she remained an outstanding student, excelling academically and graduating with high honours. However, the negative influences she had encountered over the years significantly affected her spirit and self-worth.

What stood out to me the most about Rebecca was her innate potential to achieve greatness if only she could focus her energy in the right direction. There was a fire within her—a burning desire to do more, to be more. But she was lost, unsure where to begin or how to channel that energy. She had settled for less, surrounded by people who could not see beyond mediocrity, and this stifled her growth.

I recognised that Rebecca needed someone to mentor her, help her see her worth, and guide her towards a life beyond her past mistakes. I felt compelled to help her, as her story resonated with some of my struggles. I knew our meeting was not coincidental—it was part of a more excellent plan, a divine purpose.

Helping Rebecca transform her mindset was not going to be easy. She had spent 29 years trapped in a cycle of reckless living, and breaking free from that would require significant effort and patience. But I was determined. We began praying together, and I counselled her, urging her to choose a better life. I provided her with self-development resources and encouraged her to study the scriptures, hoping that she would find strength and clarity through them.

Gradually, Rebecca began to evolve. She started believing in her purpose and letting go of the destructive habits and relationships that had held her back for so long. She fully surrendered her old life to something new, something more fulfilling.

Today, Rebecca is a completely transformed person. She leads a successful gospel music band known globally, touching lives through her music. She also hosts a talk show aimed at helping others who have lost their way, just as she once had. Her story is a powerful testament to the impact of a mindset shift. It serves as a reminder that with the proper guidance, faith, and belief in one's purpose, no obstacle is too significant to overcome. Rebecca's transformation shows the incredible power of reclaiming one's life, no matter how far gone it may seem.

However, it is essential to recognise that it takes a powerful force to change the mindset of someone profoundly shaped by the collective beliefs of their family upbringing. These influences can skew a person's perception of their purpose, often causing them to settle for less than they can achieve. Yet, with the proper guidance and support, transformation is possible.

This recalls the story of the Polgar sisters, a compelling example of how a collective family mindset can shape children's destinies. László Polgar, a Hungarian psychologist, firmly believed that "geniuses are made, not born." He set out to prove this by raising his three daughters—Susan, Sofia, and Judit—under a rigorous and focused regime centred around the game of chess.

From an early age, the Polgar sisters were immersed in an environment that prioritised intellectual development, critical thinking, and relentless practice. Chess was not just a game in their household but a way of life. Their father meticulously designed their education around chess, with each sister receiving personalised coaching, access to a wealth of chess literature, and constant opportunities to challenge their skills. The family shared a collective mindset that emphasised discipline, persistence, and the belief that extraordinary achievements were possible with the right mindset and effort.

This unwavering commitment bore fruit as all three sisters became prominent in chess. Susan became the first woman to earn the title of Grandmaster through traditional tournament play, breaking gender barriers in a male-dominated field. Sofia, known for her creativity and aggressive playstyle, was recognised as one of the strongest female players of her time. Judit, the youngest, achieved the status of the greatest female chess player in history, consistently competing against and defeating the top male players in the world.

The Polgar family's story illustrates how a collective mindset rooted in belief, purpose, and consistent effort can build individuals into extraordinary achievers. It is a testament to the power of parental influence in shaping children's potential and attitudes. When parents cultivate a mindset of excellence, perseverance, and confidence, they lay the foundation for their children to achieve greatness. The Polgar sisters' success in chess is not just a reflection of their talents but a manifestation of the collective mindset that their family nurtured.

The importance of family in shaping a child's future is so profound that even governments recognise the need to intervene when this influence becomes harmful. In the United States, the government has established a robust social service system dedicated to protecting the well-being of children. This system exists to ensure that parents do not negatively influence their children, whether through neglect, abuse, or other harmful behaviours.

The role of social services is crucial in minimising potential chaos in the future. By intervening in situations where children are at risk, they prevent the perpetuation of negative mindsets and behaviours that could have long-term detrimental effects on society. The system empowers authorities to sanction parents who misbehave in the presence of their children, whether through physical removal of the child from the home or placing them with foster parents who can provide a healthier environment.

This protective measure is not only a safeguard for the child's immediate well-being but also an investment in society's future. By ensuring that children are raised in supportive and nurturing environments, the social service system helps break dysfunctional cycles. It enables the next generation to grow up with a mindset that fosters positivity, resilience, and the potential for success.

Accessible public facilities, including ensuring that all buildings—public and commercial—are wheelchair-friendly, reflect a nation's true spirit. Likewise, social security systems that support the sick, elderly, and children demonstrate a commitment to caring for all citizens.

In a continent like Africa, which prides itself on respect and rich cultural traditions, the reality often reveals a lack of kindness, contributing to the ongoing challenges of prosperity and progress.

Developed nations' commitment to implementing and enforcing these essential services is one defining characteristic. The connection between these factors and their outcomes is clear: a nation's prosperity is not a coincidence but a result of intentional, compassionate policies and practices.

The United States' approach to child welfare through its social services is commendable. It reflects a societal commitment to safeguarding the future by ensuring that all children, regardless of their background, can grow up in an environment conducive to physical, emotional, and intellectual development. This system serves as a vital mechanism for ensuring that the collective mindset within families aligns with the broader societal values of well-being, responsibility, and the pursuit of individual potential.

Values in a nation emerge from four primary sources: religious institutions, media, educational systems, and families. Examining these streams closely is important when a country is struggling or faltering. The key to transformation lies not in wealth alone but in the values that shape society. Actual change comes from nurturing a foundation of integrity, respect, and responsibility within these core areas. Only by strengthening these values can a nation hope to thrive.

The lesson for parents is clear: the values, attitudes, and beliefs we cultivate in our homes have far-reaching implications, not just for our children but for society. By fostering a collective mindset that prioritises love, discipline, and growth, we contribute to a stronger, more harmonious future

Strategies for Fostering a Healthy and Supportive Family Environment

1. **Model Positive Behavior:** Children learn by example. Demonstrating positive attitudes, resilience, and a growth mindset can inspire them to adopt these traits.
2. **Communicate Openly:** Encourage open dialogue within the family. This fosters trust and allows children to express

their thoughts and concerns, helping them feel valued and understood.

3. **Encourage the Pursuit of Passions:** Support your children in discovering and pursuing their passions. This nurtures their talents and helps them build confidence in their abilities.

4. **Create a Nurturing Environment:** A supportive home environment prioritises learning, respect, and emotional well-being and sets the stage for children's thriving.

5. **Set Clear Expectations:** Establishing clear, consistent expectations for behaviour and effort teaches children accountability and the importance of discipline.

By embracing these strategies, parents can cultivate a family environment that supports the development of individual strengths and fosters a collective mindset aimed at growth, excellence, and fulfilment. This means going beyond the basics of care and discipline to actively shape the attitudes, values, and beliefs guiding each family member.

When parents commit to nurturing a collective mindset rooted in positivity and purpose, they create a powerful ripple effect that influences every aspect of their children's lives. The emphasis on growth encourages continuous learning and adaptation, preparing children to face challenges with resilience and determination. Focusing on excellence instils a drive to achieve personal bests, push boundaries, and expand potential. Finally, pursuing fulfilment ensures that each family member's journey is about success and finding meaning and joy in their endeavours.

In this way, the family becomes more than just a unit of individuals; it transforms into a cohesive force united by shared goals and aspirations. This collective mindset, nurtured within the family, is a foundation for lifelong success and well-being, guiding each member towards a future filled with possibility and purpose. Through intentional effort and mindful parenting, families can build a legacy of growth, excellence, and fulfilment that will endure for generations.

Parenting is not just material provisioning; it is also spiritual provisioning. God forbid we raise Hophni and Phineas—or worse, a Jezebel, male or female. Or Jeroboam, or Nadab, or Baasha, or Elah, or Omri.

> *"What we often perceive as generational curses are simply repeating patterns. We need to change the pattern to achieve different outcomes from our ancestors. The pattern is the cause and not the curse."*
> *(S. Olamilekan Isreal)*

CHAPTER 13

LOVE

Growing up, I believed that the love I experienced in my childhood and in my country was genuine. It was the only kind of love I knew, and I accepted it as the highest form of affection and care. But everything changed when I visited South Africa. During my time there, I encountered a kind of love that was completely different from what I had ever known—a love so profound and authentic that it redefined my understanding of what it means to truly love and be loved.

In South Africa, I witnessed an immeasurable love that transcended words. It was not just a feeling or a fleeting emotion; it was a way of life woven into the very fabric of their society. It was a love rooted in their history, struggles, and triumphs—a love that united people across diverse backgrounds and circumstances. I saw people caring for one another with a depth of compassion and empathy that I had never encountered before. It was a genuine, selfless love that embraced everyone, regardless of who they were or where they came from.

This experience was a revelation. It made me realise that the love I had known all my life, though sincere, was not as deep or as encompassing as the love I saw in South Africa. I had lived and been raised in an environment where expectations and conditions often limited love. But in South Africa, love was boundless. It was a force that brought people together, healed wounds, and lifted spirits. It was a love that did not just see people as they were but as they could be.

Living in South Africa transformed my mindset. It taught me that love is not just an emotion to be expressed but a powerful force to be lived every day. It showed me that true love is not about what you can receive but what you can give—how you can uplift, support, and empower those around you. This profound understanding of love has reshaped how I interact with people, how I build relationships, and how I approach life. I strive to carry that South African spirit of love with me wherever I go, sharing it in every interaction, friendship, and connection.

Returning home, I realised that this kind of love was something exceptional to my family and friends. They were taken aback by the depth and openness with which I now approached them because what seemed extraordinary to them was just a norm in South Africa. It became clear to me that one of the reasons South Africa has managed to rise above its challenges and prosper as a nation is its collective mindset of love. Despite their turbulent history, the people have chosen to hold on to love as their guiding principle, and it has been their greatest strength.

This collective love is not just a sentiment but a foundation for their society's growth and resilience. It is the reason they can overcome adversity, support each other, and build a future filled with hope and possibilities. Their definition of love is remarkable and ineffable—a love that sees beyond the self, extends a hand to others, and believes in the inherent worth of every person. It is a love that has the power to transform lives and shape nations.

My time in South Africa has taught me that love, when truly embraced as a collective mindset, is the most powerful force in the world. It could bridge divides, heal wounds, and bring out the best in humanity. It has shown me that love is not just a feeling to be felt but a way of being—a choice to see the good in others, to give without expecting in return, and to build a world where everyone is valued and supported. This is the love I strive to share wherever I go, and I am forever grateful to South Africa for showing me what it truly means to love.

Love is the most potent force in the human experience. It transcends boundaries, unites us, and has the transformative power to change individuals and societies alike. Yet, love is also one of the most elusive and misunderstood qualities. Its true essence often gets lost in translation as we try to confine it to roles, rules, and expectations. Love is simply a connection—a profound, intrinsic ability to recognise the humanity in others and extend compassion and understanding without reservation.

In this chapter, we explore how love, when embraced as a collective mindset, can uplift communities, dissolve prejudice, and foster an environment where everyone can thrive. Rosa Parks once said, "The most positive quality in the human spirit is love." This sentiment is echoed in the lives of our greatest leaders and visionaries—Martin Luther King Jr., Gandhi, and Mother Teresa—who advocated for love not just as a personal virtue but as a necessary tool for social change. They recognised that when love is expressed through "Creative, understanding goodwill for all," it becomes a powerful catalyst for unity and progress.

Rwanda: A Nation's Journey to Unity and Growth

Rwanda stands as a testament to the transformative power of love and reconciliation in the aftermath of profound national trauma. The 1994 genocide left the country shattered, with over 800,000 people killed and a nation divided along ethnic lines. Yet, in the face of this unimaginable tragedy, Rwanda chose a path of healing through love and reconciliation. Under the leadership of President Paul Kagame, the country has embarked on a remarkable journey of rebuilding not just its infrastructure but also its collective mindset.

The government instituted a series of policies aimed at fostering unity, such as abolishing ethnic identification on national identity cards and promoting a shared Rwandan identity. The establishment of the Gacaca courts, a traditional form of community justice, enabled the perpetrators of the genocide to be tried while emphasising restorative justice and reconciliation. These efforts were rooted in the belief that love, forgiveness, and mutual respect were essential to rebuilding a cohesive society.

The results of this collective mindset have been profound. Rwanda's economy has experienced significant growth, with annual GDP growth averaging around eight percent in recent years. The nation has become a model for economic development in Africa, attracting foreign investment, boosting tourism, and lifting millions out of poverty. The collective commitment to love and reconciliation has not only healed the nation but has also unleashed a wave of productivity and innovation that has transformed Rwanda into one of Africa's fastest-growing economies.

The United States: The Pursuit of the American Dream

The United States, with its rich history of diversity and immigration, has long been seen as a beacon of hope and opportunity. The American Dream—the idea that anyone, regardless of their background, can achieve success through hard work and perseverance—is deeply rooted in the country's collective mindset. This vision is fundamentally underpinned by the values of love, acceptance, and the belief in the inherent worth of every individual.

Throughout its history, the US has faced numerous challenges related to race, ethnicity, and social inequality. The civil rights movement of the 1960s, led by figures like Martin Luther King Jr., was a pivotal moment that sought to align the country's actions with its foundational ideals of liberty and justice for all. King's message of love and nonviolent resistance inspired millions to work towards a more inclusive and equitable society. His philosophy that "Hate cannot drive out hate; only love can do that" became a guiding principle in the fight for civil rights and continues to influence social justice movements today.

This commitment to diversity and inclusion has been a cornerstone of America's economic success. The US economy thrives on the contributions of people from diverse backgrounds, and its open embrace of immigrants has fostered innovation and entrepreneurship. Silicon Valley, the focal point of global technological innovation, is a prime example of this, with countless tech companies founded by immigrants who were drawn to America by the promise of opportunity and acceptance.

The collective mindset of love and inclusion has not only driven economic growth but has also made the US a global leader in science, technology, and culture. By valuing the contributions of all its citizens and fostering a spirit of collaboration and mutual respect, the United States has created a society where individuals are empowered to reach their full potential, thereby contributing to the nation's overall prosperity.

Nigeria: The Struggles of a Divided Mindset

Nigeria, on the other hand, serves as an example of how the absence of a collective love mindset can hinder a nation's potential. As Africa's most populous country, rich in natural resources and cultural diversity, Nigeria should be a beacon of economic strength and unity on the continent. However, the nation continues to struggle with deep-seated issues of disunity, corruption, and economic instability, primarily due to the lack of a cohesive, collective mindset centred on love and common purpose.

One of the critical challenges Nigeria faces is its fragmented sense of national identity. The country is divided along ethnic, religious, and regional lines, with each group often prioritising its interests over the common good. This division has created an environment of mistrust and competition rather than cooperation and unity. The absence of a collective love mindset means that people are more likely to view those outside their group with suspicion or hostility, which has fueled conflicts and hindered national development.

This division is particularly evident in Nigeria's political landscape, where choosing the right leaders is often clouded by biases based on ethnicity and religion rather than competence and vision. The electorate is frequently influenced by these divisive factors, leading to the election of leaders who do not necessarily represent the best interests of the nation as a whole. This lack of unity and collective purpose has allowed corruption to flourish, with leaders often prioritising personal gain over the welfare of the people. As a result, the nation's resources are mismanaged, and opportunities for growth are squandered.

The impact of this collective non-love mindset is also evident in Nigeria's economic performance. Despite its vast oil wealth and a large, youthful population, Nigeria struggles to achieve its potential as one of Africa's leading economies. High levels of poverty, unemployment, and inequality persist, exacerbated by systemic corruption and poor governance. The lack of a shared vision for the country means that efforts to build a strong, diversified economy are undermined by conflicting interests and a focus on short-term gains rather than sustainable development.

Nigeria deserves to be among the greatest economies in Africa, if not the world. With its abundant natural resources, vibrant entrepreneurial spirit, and dynamic cultural heritage, the country has all the ingredients for success. However, without a collective love mindset that holds unity, integrity, and the well-being of all its citizens in high regard, these potential strengths remain untapped. The divisions and distrust that pervade society prevent Nigerians from working together towards a shared future of prosperity and peace.

For Nigeria to realise its true potential, there must be a fundamental shift in mindset. A collective love mindset—where people see beyond their differences, work together for the common good, and hold their leaders accountable—can transform the nation. This requires a commitment to fostering unity, embracing diversity, and building trust across all levels of society. By cultivating a shared vision of love, respect, and cooperation, Nigeria can overcome its challenges and emerge as a powerful force for good in Africa and the world.

The Economic and Social Benefits of a Loving Mindset

Rwanda and the United States, though vastly different in their histories and contexts, both demonstrate the powerful impact of adopting a mindset of love and reconciliation. In Rwanda, a commitment to forgiveness and unity has transformed a once-divided nation into a beacon of economic hope and social stability in Africa. In the United States, the embrace of diversity and the belief in the dignity and potential of every individual has fueled decades of innovation and economic growth.

When a collective mindset is grounded in love, it becomes a powerful tool for social transformation. It inspires us to look beyond ourselves, to serve others, and to build communities where everyone feels valued and supported. Love is not passive; it requires active participation, a commitment to empathy, and a willingness to embrace others despite our differences. It is this mindset that has the potential to heal, unite, and elevate humanity to its highest potential.

As **Martin Luther King Jr.** so aptly put it, "Darkness cannot drive out darkness; only light can do that. Hate cannot drive out hate; only love can do that." By choosing to love without expectation, to connect without judgment, and to act with compassion, we become the architects of a brighter, more inclusive future. This is the power of love, the most transformative force in the universe, and the cornerstone of a truly resilient collective mindset.

"Having a collective love mindset shouldn't just be a sentiment, but it's a foundation for every societal growth and resilience."
(S. Olamilekan Isreal)

CHAPTER 14

SUSTAINABILITY

Sustainability is not just a trendy term; it represents a fundamental change in how we engage with the world around us. My understanding of this concept did not come from books or lectures but from real-life experiences, mainly through my travels. Seeing how different countries approached sustainability gave me a new perspective. In many developed nations, sustainability is not just a set of rules or practices; it is a deeply ingrained mindset.

A sustainability mindset goes beyond simply recognising environmental challenges; it involves a profound understanding of the interconnectedness of ecological balance, social equity, and economic prosperity. It calls for intentional choices that consider the long-term effects of our actions on the planet, communities, and future generations.

Developing this mindset starts with defining personal or organisational values that prioritise environmental stewardship and societal well-being. Knowing the purpose behind these values serves as a guiding compass, helping us navigate challenges and remain committed to sustainability goals.

A sustainability mindset thrives on innovation and adaptability. It encourages creative problem-solving and the exploration of new technologies and approaches that foster positive change while minimising environmental impact.

Sustainability is inherently a collective effort rooted in empathy and collaboration. Engaging with diverse stakeholders and actively listening to their perspectives allows us to co-create sustainable solutions that benefit everyone.

Examples of this mindset in action include:

- Interface, a global carpet manufacturer, launched its Mission Zero initiative to eliminate negative environmental impacts by 2020.
- Narayana Peesapaty invented edible cutlery made from millet, promoting sustainability and reducing single-use plastic waste in India.
- Ugly Juice rescues "ugly" and surplus fruits, transforming

them into nutritious cold-pressed juices. Thus, it reduces food waste and advances sustainability.

Events like the COP26 climate summit highlight the collaborative efforts of nations to address climate change, uniting in a sustainability mindset to seek global solutions. By embracing these principles, we can work together to build a more sustainable future for all.

I want my children to grow up in a world where sustainability is as natural as breathing and part of everyday life. This goes beyond caring for the environment—it is about creating a world where doing good and achieving success are not opposing goals. **Harvard Business School** sums this up nicely with **"Doing Well and Doing Good,"** showing that financial success and social responsibility can and should go hand in hand.

Where I grew up, though, the focus was almost entirely on Money. Success is measured by the amount of money in your bank account, often without considering the social or environmental costs. Money is undoubtedly essential, but it should not come at the expense of our planet or communities. That is where the sustainability mindset changes everything— it redefines what true success looks like.

The Need for a Mindset Shift

An experience that crystallised the importance of sustainability for me occurred a few years ago at a grocery store. I had been buying my two-year-old daughter a particular fruit juice brand for some time. On this day, however, when I poured the juice into her cup, I noticed that the colour was off and strange particles were in it. Alarmed, I immediately returned to the store to report the issue. The manager, however, was indifferent, brushing off my concerns by blaming the supplier. This lack of accountability was shocking. What if my daughter had consumed that juice?

This incident is emblematic of a more significant problem— one that extends beyond faulty products. It highlights a pervasive mindset in many parts of the world where the purpose of business is misunderstood. Profit is prioritised over the well-being of consumers and the environment. Before this incident, I had encountered fake medications, substandard body creams, and other defective household products. These experiences are all too common and persist mainly because of weak consumer protection regulations. In many places, if you purchase a faulty product, there is little you can do—no one seems to care.

Defining Sustainability

So, what is sustainability? At its core, sustainability is about meeting the needs of the present without compromising the ability of future generations to meet their own needs. In business, this means operating in a way that does not harm the environment, community, or society. It is about making a positive impact and ensuring that your actions today contribute to a better tomorrow.

According to Harvard Business School, businesses should consider the "triple bottom line," which assesses the impact of a company's actions on profit, people, and the planet. A business that does not operate with this framework is not truly sustainable. This approach encourages companies to go beyond financial success and consider their social and environmental impact.

But sustainability is not simply for businesses; it also applies to individuals. "Individual Sustainability" is about being responsible, transparent, and mindful of your impact on the environment, economy, and society. It is about creating harmony, fostering interconnection, and cultivating self-awareness in your values, thoughts, behaviours, and actions. Imagine growing up in a city where sustainability is not valued; it is considered irrelevant, and opposite behaviours are accepted as the norm. This was my experience—a place where most people are unaware of the benefits of sustainability and thus act without consideration. But change begins with awareness, and from awareness comes action.

The Collective Mindset and Society

Adopting a sustainability mindset is not just an individual responsibility; it is a collective one. The impact can be profound when entire communities, businesses, and governments embrace this mindset. This collective mindset is crucial in shaping our future, influencing how we think and act in everything we do. A society prioritising sustainability will naturally foster businesses, practices, and policies that reflect these values.

Governments have a significant role to play. When a government adopts a sustainability mindset, the effects ripple throughout society. Policies that prioritise renewable energy, sustainable agriculture, and green technology protect the environment and promote economic growth and social equity. By setting standards and regulations, governments can encourage businesses and individuals to adopt more sustainable practices, creating a positive feedback loop that benefits everyone.

Examples of Sustainability in Action

Finland is a prime example of a country that has fully embraced a sustainability mindset. Ranked as one of the most sustainable countries in the world, Finland's approach to sustainability is comprehensive, encompassing everything from energy production to education. The country's commitment to renewable energy, sustainable forestry, and waste reduction has preserved its natural resources and bolstered its economy. Finland's education system, which integrates sustainability into the curriculum from a young age, ensures that future generations will continue prioritising these values.

IKEA, the global furniture giant, is another example of an organisation that has made sustainability a core part of its business model. IKEA's journey towards sustainability began with the realisation that their business practices significantly impacted the environment. In response, they set ambitious goals to use only renewable and recycled materials in their products by 2030. This commitment to sustainability has reduced their environmental footprint and enhanced their brand reputation and customer loyalty. IKEA's success demonstrates that a sustainability mindset can drive innovation, reduce costs, and create long-term value for the company and society.

Google's Chief Sustainability Officer, Kate Brandt, has been instrumental in embedding sustainability into the company's culture. Under her leadership, Google has committed to operating entirely on carbon-free energy by 2030 and has already achieved carbon neutrality. Brandt's work at Google shows how a sustainability mindset can be integrated into a company's operations at every level, driving environmental and economic benefits.

Mohammed Jameel Al Ramaha, the CEO of Masdar, has also been a key figure in promoting sustainability. Masdar, based in the United Arab Emirates, is a global leader in renewable energy and sustainable urban development. Under Al Ramaha's leadership, Masdar has expanded its portfolio to include solar, wind, and waste-to-energy projects, contributing to the UAE's goal of increasing the share of clean energy in its total energy mix. Al Ramaha's vision for Masdar highlights the potential for businesses to lead the way in the global transition to a sustainable future.

Embedding Sustainability into Culture

To truly embed sustainability into a group's culture, whether in business, government, or society, requires a shift in mindset at all levels. Here are some strategies for achieving this:

1. **Education and Awareness:** Sustainability should be integrated into education from a young age, ensuring that future generations understand its importance. Businesses and governments should also invest in training programs to educate employees and citizens about sustainable practices.

2. **Leadership Commitment:** Leaders must lead by example and demonstrate a commitment to sustainability in their actions and decisions. This includes setting clear goals, measuring progress, and holding themselves and others accountable.

3. **Incentives and Regulations:** Governments can encourage sustainable practices through incentives, such as tax breaks for renewable energy investments and regulations that require businesses to adhere to environmental standards.

4. **Innovation and Collaboration:** Sustainability often requires new ways of thinking and doing. Encouraging innovation and collaboration across sectors can lead to developing new technologies and practices that benefit everyone.

5. **Community Engagement:** Building a culture of sustainability requires the involvement of the entire community. Initiatives that engage citizens in sustainability efforts, such as recycling programs or community gardens, can help to foster a sense of collective responsibility.

The Impact of a Sustainability Mindset

Adopting a sustainability mindset has a far-reaching impact. Environmentally, it leads to preserving natural resources, reducing pollution, and a healthier planet. Socially, it promotes equity, reduces inequality, and enhances the quality of life for all citizens. Economically, it drives innovation, creates jobs, and ensures long-term prosperity.

In conclusion, sustainability is not just a buzzword or a passing trend; it is a mindset that needs to be embraced by everyone, from individuals to entire societies. When we adopt this mindset, we create a world where doing the right thing and succeeding go hand in hand. The examples of Finland, IKEA, Kate Brandt, and Mohammed Jameel Al Ramaha show us that committing to sustainability brings lasting and meaningful benefits.

It is up to us—both as individuals and as a collective—to carry this mindset forward. Doing so can shape a better world for future generations, one where sustainability is the norm and our actions today lead to a brighter tomorrow.

"If we are not collectively thinking about sustainability, then we cannot impact the world to be better"
(S. Olamilekan Isreal)

LEGACY

How do we want to be perceived—as individuals, organisations, or in society? What do we truly hope people will say about us at our funeral? Some might brush off these questions with a casual "Who cares?" Yet, these are among the most profound questions we must ask ourselves, whether as individuals or as leaders.

Stephen Covey wisely stated, "If you want your leadership to have meaning truly, you need to consider the Law of Legacy. Why? Because a leader's lasting value is measured by succession." Similarly, Chris Musgrove reminds us, "Success is not measured by what you're leaving to, but by what you are leaving behind."

Legacy is not merely what we leave behind; it is how we are remembered, the influence that endures, and the values that continue to shape the world long after we are gone. For groups and organisations, legacy reflects the collective mindset that guided them—what they believed, how they acted, and the impact they sought to create. A shared vision, deeply held values, and a unified purpose can forge a legacy that resonates through the ages.

This chapter delves into how collective mindsets shape a group's legacy, drawing on powerful examples such as the Suffragettes, Greenpeace, Mother Teresa, Jesus and his disciples, and other prophets who left an indelible mark on history. Their stories testify to the enduring power of a unified vision and the impact a collective mindset can have on the world.

From Nelson Mandela's visionary leadership, which united a fractured nation, to Joan of Arc's indomitable spirit, which inspired armies to triumph against overwhelming odds, these remarkable individuals have left an enduring mark on our collective consciousness.

Their courage, charisma, and unwavering determination exemplify what it means to lead with purpose and inspire others to achieve greatness. Throughout history, countless leaders have shaped our societies and left lasting legacies. Among them is Mahatma Gandhi, the father of Indian independence.

Gandhi's nonviolent resistance inspired millions, leading to India's liberation from British rule. His emphasis on peaceful protest and civil disobedience highlighted the power of moral leadership and the potential for change without violence. Gandhi's steadfast commitment to justice and equality is a timeless reminder of the transformative impact one individual can have.

Steve Jobs, co-founder of Apple Inc., was another visionary leader who revolutionised the technology industry. His ability to anticipate consumer needs and create innovative products set him apart as a transformative figure. Jobs' relentless pursuit of excellence and meticulous attention to detail resulted in iconic products like the iPhone and MacBook, fundamentally changing how we live and work.

In addition to political and social leaders, military leaders have also significantly shaped history. Alexander the Great and Julius Caesar are notable examples of demonstrating exceptional military prowess and strategic thinking.

Alexander, the Macedonian king, is celebrated for his military conquests and for creating one of the largest empires in history. His leadership inspired deep loyalty among his troops, and his innovative tactics and personal bravery on the battlefield earned him respect and admiration. Alexander's ability to lead by example and his relentless pursuit of victory offer valuable lessons in effective leadership.

Julius Caesar, the Roman general and statesman, exemplified formidable leadership qualities. His military campaigns and political manoeuvres transformed the Roman Republic into the Roman Empire. His famous words, **"Veni, Vidi, Vici"** ("I came, I saw, I conquered"), reflect his decisive approach and ability to inspire loyalty among his soldiers and allies. Caesar's adaptability in the face of changing circumstances and his capacity to make tough decisions highlight strong leadership's profound impact in times of uncertainty.

These leaders remind us that the essence of authentic leadership lies not just in authority but in the ability to inspire, uplift, and effect meaningful change.

The Suffragettes: A Legacy of Equality and Empowerment

The Suffragettes were a group of courageous women who fought tirelessly for women's right to vote in the early 20th century. Their collective mindset was rooted in a profound belief in equality and justice. They were determined to challenge the societal norms that relegated women to a secondary status, and they pursued their goal with unwavering resolve, even in the face of persecution, imprisonment, and violence.

The Suffragettes' legacy is one of empowerment and social change. Their efforts led to the eventual recognition of women's suffrage in many countries, fundamentally altering the course of history. However, their legacy goes beyond the right to vote; they inspired future generations to continue the fight for gender equality and to challenge injustice in all its forms. The collective mindset of the Suffragettes—marked by resilience, courage, and a commitment to justice—has left a lasting impact that continues to influence movements for equality today.

Greenpeace: A Legacy of Environmental Stewardship

Greenpeace, founded in the early 1970s, is an environmental organisation synonymous with the fight to protect the planet. Its collective mindset is characterised by a deep respect for nature, a sense of urgency in addressing environmental threats, and a belief in the power of direct action to bring about change.

Greenpeace's legacy is one of environmental stewardship and activism. Their campaigns have led to significant victories, such as banning commercial whaling, reducing toxic waste dumping, and protecting endangered species. But perhaps even more importantly, Greenpeace has succeeded in raising global awareness about environmental issues and inspiring millions of people to act. The collective mindset of Greenpeace—driven by a passion for the environment and a commitment to nonviolent activism—has created a legacy that continues to influence environmental policies and movements worldwide.

Mother Teresa: A Legacy of Compassion and Collective Mindset

Mother Teresa's leadership offers a profound example of how one individual can leave a legacy that transcends time, shaping the collective mindset of an entire society. Her life was a testament to the power of compassion, humility, and unwavering commitment to serving the most vulnerable.

Born in 1910 in what North Macedonia is now, Mother Teresa dedicated her life to caring for the poor, sick, and dying, particularly in the slums of Calcutta, India. Her selfless acts of kindness and tireless work to alleviate suffering captured the world's attention and inspired countless others to follow her example.

The legacy she left behind was not just the establishment of the Missionaries of Charity. This congregation continues to serve people in need across the globe, but also the creation of a collective mindset rooted in empathy and service. Mother Teresa's approach to leadership was grounded in love and a deep sense of responsibility towards those less fortunate. Her belief that **"Not all of us can do great things, but we can do small things with great love"** resonated with people from all walks of life, encouraging a societal shift towards caring for others, regardless of their background or circumstances.

Her legacy continues to influence how we think about service, charity, and the role of compassion in leadership. The collective mindset that emerged from her work values human dignity, prioritises the needs of the marginalised, and recognises that authentic leadership is not about power or prestige but about making a meaningful difference in the lives of others.

Today, the ripple effect of Mother Teresa's leadership is evident in numerous charitable organisations, movements, and individual actions that seek to alleviate suffering and promote kindness. By embodying the principles she lived by, society has adopted a collective mindset that values compassion, service, and the inherent worth of every person.

Jesus and His Disciples: A Legacy of Faith and Compassion

The story of Jesus and His disciples is one of the most potent examples of how a collective mindset can shape a legacy that endures for millennia. Jesus, through His teachings and actions, instilled in His disciples a mindset centred on faith, love, and compassion. He emphasised the importance of serving others, forgiving those who wronged them, and spreading God's love.

The legacy of Jesus and His disciples is the foundation of Christianity, a faith that has profoundly influenced the world for over two thousand years. Their collective mindset has inspired countless individuals to live lives of service, to seek justice for the oppressed, and to spread compassion and love. The teachings of Jesus, as carried forward by His disciples and later prophets, have shaped cultures, laws, and societies, leaving a legacy that continues to guide millions of people in their daily lives.

Steps to Ensure a Lasting Legacy

Creating a legacy, like that of the Suffragettes, Greenpeace, and Jesus and His disciples, requires more than just passion and effort. It demands a deliberate and sustained focus on cultivating a collective mindset that aligns with the desired impact. Here are steps that groups and organisations can take to ensure the longevity and positive influence of their collective mindset:

1. **Define a Clear Vision and Purpose:** A legacy begins with a clear and compelling vision. Groups must articulate what they stand for and what they aim to achieve. This vision should be deeply rooted in values that resonate with current members and future generations.

2. **Cultivate a Strong Collective Identity:** A group's legacy's strength is tied to its collective identity's strength. This

identity should be built on shared values, beliefs, and practices that unite members and give them a sense of belonging and purpose.

3. **Lead by Example:** A group's leaders' actions play a crucial role in shaping its legacy. Leaders must embody the group's values and principles, setting an example for others to follow. Their actions should reflect the collective mindset the group wishes to instil in future generations.

4. **Foster Inclusivity and Adaptability:** Groups must be inclusive and adaptable to ensure a legacy. They should welcome new members and perspectives and be willing to evolve and preserve the group's legacy and ability, allowing it to remain relevant and impactful over time.

5. **Document and Share the Story:** Storytelling is an essential element of legacy-building. Groups should document their history, achievements, and lessons learnt and share these stories with others. This not only preserves the group's legacy but also inspires future generations to carry it forward.

6. **Invest in Future Leaders:** A legacy requires cultivating future leaders who will carry the torch. Groups should invest in the development of their members, providing mentorship, training, and opportunities for growth. Empowering the next generation ensures the group's collective mindset and impact endure.

The legacy of a group or organisation reflects its collective mindset—a testament to what it believed, how it acted, and the impact it sought to create. The stories of the Suffragettes, Greenpeace, and Jesus and His disciples demonstrate the profound and lasting influence a unified vision, shared values, and determined action can have on the world.

By cultivating a collective mindset rooted in purpose, driven by passion, and adaptable to change, groups can create a legacy that not only endures but continues to inspire and shape the future.

"Success is not measured by what you're leaving to, but by what you are leaving behind." (Chris Musgrove)

APPRECIATION

Dear Reader,

As you embark on this journey through the pages of this book, I am filled with anticipation for the transformation it can bring to your life, your organisation, and our society. Your engagement with these words breathes life into them, and I wholeheartedly believe that each chapter will resonate deeply with you.

This book is more than just a collection of ideas; it catalyses change. I hope it inspires you, instils a renewed sense of purpose, and ignites a passion for transformation in every aspect of your life. Your journey towards personal growth, organisational success, and societal improvement begins here.

I encourage you to share the insights you have gained with your loved ones. Your recommendations not only foster a culture of growth but also help to minimise confusion and disconnection in our society. By introducing this book to those around you, you contribute to a ripple effect of positive change—one that transcends individual lives and touches communities.

I invite you to connect with me through my other writings and daily inspirations. Follow us on our website, Instagram, Facebook, and LinkedIn to stay updated on our latest posts and news. Your feedback is invaluable, and I look forward to hearing your thoughts and the challenges you face along your journey.

Thank you for investing your time in this book. May it bring joy, wisdom, and practical solutions that empower you to act, pursue your dreams, and lead a purposeful life.

With heartfelt gratitude,

S. Olamilekan Isreal

ACKNOWLEDGMENT

I express my deepest gratitude to the King of the Universe and the Holy Spirit for granting me the wisdom, insight, strength, and grace to bring this book to life. Amid one of the most challenging economic situations my country has faced in the last 16 years, I found the courage and resilience to see this project through. Without divine guidance, this book would have remained an idea, never brought to fruition.

To my beloved team, thank you for your unwavering support and motivation. Your constant encouragement gave me the strength to keep writing despite the challenging journey. I wish you all the universe's favour as you continue your life paths.

I extend my heartfelt appreciation to my loving wife, whose steadfast support and encouragement sustained me throughout the writing process. Her belief in this project gave me the courage to push forward. To my dear friend who urged me to write on this subject after hearing me speak about it, thank you for your foresight and belief in the message. Your suggestion has indeed impacted many lives, and I am forever grateful.

To Mr. Kolade Gbolagade, my incredible editor, I owe a debt of gratitude. Your commitment, feedback, and belief in this work have enriched every page. Thank you for always being there whenever I needed guidance and for your dedication to making this project the best possible.

I also want to thank my friends and family for their endless love and support during this journey. Your belief in me kept my spirit high. To those whose names I may not have mentioned, your contributions have not gone unnoticed. Each of you significantly shaped this work, and I am immensely thankful for that.

Lastly, I would like to thank myself for my resilience, determination, and unwavering pursuit of this dream. This journey has been one of growth, perseverance, and transformation, and I am proud to have reached this point.

With sincere gratitude,

S. Olamilekan Isreal